The Independent Golfer's Guide to the Highlands and Islands Of Scotland

TIG

The Independent Golfer's Guide to the Highlands and Islands Of Scotland

Willis Copeland

A *TIG* Book

ISBN 1-59975-751-6

Published by The Independent Golfer
644 Calle de los Amigos, Suite 7
Santa Barbara, CA 93105

Cover photo courtesy of Golf Highland and Durness Golf Club

To my beautiful bride of 32 years, Susan, without whom this book would have remained only a dream.

I am indebted to all the Scots, living and passed on, whose keen sense of fair play, sportsmanship and love of competition combined with the their country's magnificent geography to create for us the game that we love.

I am also thankful to my American golfing buddies who put up with far too many interruptions in their Scottish golf so that I could gather yet more material for this book.

Contents

1. I'm Looking for Something Special 1

2. This Land Was Specially Designed by the
    Almighty to Play Golf 11

3. When in Scotland, Play As the Scots Play 23

4. Do Ye Ha a Time? 55

5. Play Golf and Save Money: Two Great
    Scottish Traditions 71

6. First, Look Right 87

7. Bide a Wee 97

8. Gie Her a Haggis 105

9. Four Seasons in One Day 113

10. Featheries, Gutties and Hickory Shafts 119

11. Scotland Beyond the Courses 127

12. Mina Berrn 145

13. On Ye Go 153

    Appendix A – Sample *Caddienote* 157

    Index 163

CHAPTER I

I'm Looking for Something Local.

It turned out to be a most convivial evening among strangers. I had wandered into the Eagle Hotel's bar in the evening after a sixteen-hour flight from Los Angeles to Edinburgh, Scotland, and then a four-hour car ride north to the village of Dornoch on the East Coast of the Scottish Highlands. My wife was back in our Bed and Breakfast accommodations, having gone straight to bed after being awake for 24 hours. But I hadn't wanted to sleep. My way of fighting jet lag is to force myself to be on local time and, since it was early evening and I didn't want to go to bed until at least 11:00 p.m., I had decided to go for a walk and check out the local drinking establishments.

It was a slow night in the Eagle, an unusual situation for early July. Locals and visitors who know about it enjoy the Eagle's friendly atmosphere. The owner's collection of prints of old golfing scenes, strange farming implements, empty bottles of unusual wines and spirits, and the jokes and cartoons that cover the walls seem to grow bigger and more cluttered every time I return. The staff is always very friendly, the food quite good, and the selection of beer and whiskey is typically Scottish pub. That is, it is broad and varied.

It was therefore a bit unusual to find just three patrons in the bar this evening. Two fellows were sitting at the bar, talking quietly. A third was lounging in a booth by himself, nursing his lager while the bartender polished glasses with one eye on a rugby match on the television. As I sipped my single malt whiskey (I know they say whiskey is bad for jet lag but, heck, I was in Scotland), I overheard the two locals at the bar discussing the possibility that David Beckham, the most popular footballer (soccer player) in Europe might be traded from Manchester United, the club for which he had played since the age of 14, to Real Madrid, an opponent of United's in the European Club Championships.

Surprised to hear about this possibility, I broke into the conversation by asking about this pending trade. My American forwardness didn't seem to bother these two Scots, and we talked about British soccer, Beckham, and his wife Victoria (the former Posh Spice of the Spice Girls) for a bit until one of the fellows asked if I was in Scotland on holiday. "Sort of," I answered. "Playing golf is both holiday and work for me."

When I described to them my goal of playing and writing about as many of the courses in the Highlands and Islands as I could, they got excited. Harry and Alistair were both golfers themselves and were eager to hear what I thought of the courses I had played. Assuming that I was talking to Dornoch locals, I immediately offered that there was none finer than the Royal Dornoch Championship course. After all, it was just a few hundred yards from where we sat. Harry, a thin older fellow with the ruddiness of North Sea winters in his face, smiled, contented to have confirmed what he already knew to be God's own truth. "Aye. You'll no find a better test o' golf than this one right here," he proudly laughed. Alistair, younger and broader than his drinking buddy, quickly agreed. "Aye. There's none finer."

But what of the other courses in the area, he wanted to know. Had I played Tain or Golspie? What about Brora? All of them were within 30 minutes drive of the village of Dornoch, and all were well known and frequently played by local golfers.

I was happy to admit that I knew them all, and we shared stories about each. Harry asked if I recalled the approach to the 18th green at Brora. I sure did. I had to admit hitting my shot just a bit short and suffering the ignominy of having my ball roll back down the hill into the collection area 30 yards off the green, while members watched and smiled knowingly from the

Courtesy Golf Highlands

Hole #1 "Achincharter" at Royal Dornoch's Championship Course, surrounded on three sides by blooming gorse. Hole #2 "Sutherland" and the North Sea are to the right.

window of the clubhouse bar that overlooked the 18th green. Harry assured me that this was a common plight of visiting players to Brora, and a never-ending source of entertainment to the members safely ensconced in their warm clubhouse.

Harry recalled for a bashful Alistair his triumph three years back at Tain, where he had played well in a competition against the TOFF's (The Tain Over Fifty-Five club). This friendly rivalry among "senior" golfers throughout the area is, I was told, a continuing source of pleasure for those "a bit longer in the tooth."

Then the conversation moved to even lesser known courses. Alistair wanted to know if I had driven the #1 hole at Strathpeffer Spa? No? I really should, he remarked. It is said to have the longest drop from tee to fairway landing area of any golf hole in the UK. What about Durness? Did I know it? Yes, I had played it, the most northern course on the UK mainland. Neither Harry nor Alistair had played it, but they both knew about its #9 hole, as apparently did every golfer in Scotland. They wanted to know how I liked hitting my tee shot from the edge of a precipice, across an open expanse of the Atlantic Ocean to a green perched on an opposite cliff beyond. They chuckled when I described how far right of the green I confessed to aiming that shot so that it could not possibly go left and end in the sea.

As our conversation grew more animated, Harry offered to buy me another single malt. I knew full well that, if I accepted, social necessity would oblige me to buy a round as well. As the Scots say, it would be "My shout." Of course, that would also be followed by another from Alistair. A "yes" to Harry would mean that it would be at least three rounds before I could get out of the Eagle. But the conversation was interesting. Sure, why not!

As our sharing of northern Scottish courses continued – some of which one or more of us had played, others which we all had just heard about – the other lone Eagle patron listened from his booth. I had noticed that he was following our conversation with obvious growing interest. To include him, I asked if he played golf and what courses he had played. It turned out that Chas was an American, too, and had just played Royal Dornoch that day. Harry especially was pleased to hear how much he had enjoyed his round. Chas had three days left of a nine-day golfing tour that had already taken him and fifteen other Americans and Canadians to five of the more well-known (to North Americans) courses in Scotland – Prestwick, Royal Troon, Carnoustie, Nairn, and now Royal Dornoch. The two courses he had yet to play on his tour were the Old and Jubilee courses at St. Andrews.

We talked about the courses he had played for a time, but Chas was more interested in the other courses we had been sharing stories about earlier. He had no idea that these courses existed. When I pointed out Scotland boasted 546 golf courses, many of world-class rank, Chas was astounded. He had no idea that, in the most scenic Highlands and Islands of Scotland's north alone, any golfer could play 88 of these courses without the hassle of making reservations months ahead, and at green fee rates that were fractions of what he was paying on his tour. This was a whole world of golf he hadn't known existed. Were they all as good as the ones we had been discussing? No, not all, we agreed. Some were short and poorly maintained, intended to serve only local golfers. But many others were "highland golf gems" located in wild and glorious mountain or seaside settings. These courses were every bit as wonderful as those more well-known to Americans. (They just weren't venues for the only Scottish golf that most Americans know about, the British Open.) Nevertheless, they do offer marvelously differing golf experiences to visiting golfers willing to venture off the well-trod tour paths.

Ah, yes, the "golfing experience" thing. Chas admitted that he was less than satisfied with the experience he had been having on his tour. Sure, the golf was great. We all agreed that we would each love to play any of the courses that his tour had taken him to. But he had hoped that the golfing experience would be more than just the golf. He had spent the past six days traveling with a bus load of Americans and Canadians from course to hotel to course. They had played together, eaten together, been glad-handed and entertained together, but seldom had they interacted with Scots beyond the hotel and course staff. They had played golf on some of the courses best known to Americans, and typically had their own countrymen playing ahead of and behind them. And they had paid handsomely to do so. Chas volunteered that his tour had cost him and his golfing buddy $4,200 each, plus incidental expenses and gratuities, and there were plenty of those. For this they would play 18 holes on each of eight different courses, stay nine nights in three different hotels, eat 29 meals, travel on 18 bus trips, and sit through three "Evenings of Scottish Entertainment" in their hotel bars.

But this evening, Chas had had enough of the tour thing and had "broken away" from his group. His buddy and all the other tour members were at the big tourist hotel on the other side of the village, listening to Donny Stewart, self-styled

Courtesy Golf Highlands

Sunset on the Boat of Garten Golf Course with the Grampian Mountains in the background

"Chieftain of Scottish Music." Donny, resplendent in silver hair, Scottish plaid trousers and a powder-blue sport coat, played electronic keyboard in the hotel's bar for its guests. Supported by his electronic rhythm box, Donny offered an eclectic mixture of Scottish standards (*Banks of Loch Lomond*, *Westering Home*) and dated American pop (*Tie a Yellow Ribbon Around the Old Oak Tree*, *Sweet Caroline*). Seeking refuge from Donny's melodies, Chas had walked the village looking for "something local" and chanced upon at the Eagle Hotel.

Finding people like us was what he had hoped for throughout his golfing tour of Scotland. We offered him the opportunity to sit with local golfers and talk local golf. This night at the Eagle Hotel, Chas learned of the great array of courses in the Scottish North. He learned that, had he and his buddy not been attached to a tour, they could have played any of these magnificent courses as they wished.

Had they been Independent Golfers, not tied to their tour, Chas and his buddies could have sought out lesser-known and much less crowded but equally spectacular courses. If they had enjoyed themselves on a particular course, they could have stayed for another eighteen. As Independent Golfers, they could have followed a morning round with lunch, perhaps a steak pie or fish and chips in a local pub or homemade soup and a toasted ham and cheese sandwich in a small restaurant, and then driven 45 minutes over an extraordinarily scenic road that winds through mountains, forests, and fields to play a different but equally challenging course in the afternoon. They could have stayed at a small but comfortable Bed and Breakfast, where they could have chatted with the owners over an evening cup of tea or wandered down the road to the local pub instead of spending all their waking hours in the company of fellow tour members. And they could have done all this at a fraction of the $4,200 that they had paid for their tour. These are the possibilities open to American golfers who are willing to travel independently.

Tour companies offer a service, and they charge accordingly. They are happy to bus you to a selected number of Scotland's more well-known, and more crowded, courses. They will bundle you with fellow tourists from Milwaukee or Houston onto the tees and into the hotels. They will probably spice the trip up with an evening floorshow of bagpipe playing and they might even throw in a tour of a whiskey distillery. For this they will charge you handsomely, and claim to have given you the "golfing experience of a lifetime in Scotland." If this is what you are looking for then go to a travel agent, select a tour package, pay your money, and enjoy the experience.

But if you join a tour, you will never get to play some of the most fabulous courses in Scotland, the courses of the Highlands and Islands. This most wondrous and scenic of all Scottish regions offers courses that rival any in the British Isles. Some are ranked at or near the top of any number of "best-courses-in-the-world" lists. Most are very old and offer an almost mystical sense of contact with the roots of the game. All exist for the enjoyment of local Scots, are not crowded with tourists, and present the opportunity to play over ground hallowed by the Greats of the past. Tours don't include these courses because Americans don't see them on their televisions and so don't ask to play them.

If you join a tour, you will also never get to play golf with a Scot. You won't be invited down to the local pub for a pub lunch and a pint of lager or a "bump of the bogwater." You won't sit and talk golf into the wee hours with locals whose great-great-grandparents knew every bunker, swale, and fairway bump of the course you just played that afternoon. You won't be able to stand on an elevated tee and gaze across grass-tufted dunes toward the sea with a view that is uncluttered by busy foursomes working their way in lock-step around the course in front of you. You won't be able, on a whim, to return the next day to that course that baffled you so, this time to test your suspicion that a drive down the left side of the fairway on the third hole is the real way to come into the green with a doable approach.

In short, that expensive golf package tour will let you play some famous Scottish courses but it will not give you the opportunity to experience the true golf of Scotland.

It may be that, for you, the golf experience must include wild and wonderful scenery not overrun by tourists. You may believe that the need to meet different shot demands for each hole defines an important quality of the courses you like to play. The history and traditions of the game may never be far from your mind. Golf, for you, may be the challenge of selecting between two shots, one with greater potential reward but also greater risk. You may like the freedom and independence of controlling your own schedule, of deciding when you will play, where you will play, and with whom you will play the game you love. If all this is important to you, then you are, at heart, an Independent Golfer, and playing golf independently in the Highlands and Islands of Scotland is something you cannot miss in this life.

You may never have considered a golfing holiday in Scotland as a realistic possibility for yourself or your friends. If you are like most American golfers, you have heard stories of golf in Scotland as being wonderfully entertaining, "the trip of a lifetime," or even a mystical experience. But also, like most Americans, you probably know few specifics about Scottish golf possibilities beyond what you see every July on televised segments associated with the British Open. You probably have heard of a handful of the most well-known Scottish courses but, like Chas in the Eagle Hotel, you are not aware of the great range of other courses available for play there. Also, for you, a golfing trip to Scotland may appear to be impractical or beyond your budget. After all, you could play a lot of golf in Arizona, the Carolinas, the Monterey Peninsula, or Hawaii for the $4,200 that Chas and his buddies each paid for their seven rounds in Scotland.

If you are an Independent Golfer, then the information in the pages that follow is exactly what you need to enjoy golf in Scotland, free of the limitations of tour travel and at a fraction of the cost that you would pay the tour companies. You will read about the nature of Scottish golf and the customs for play there, about reserving tee times when necessary (and about why it is easy and often not even necessary to do so), and about how to plan your trip so that you will need to spend much less money than the typical "tour-packaged" golfer does.

You will read about traveling in Scotland – transportation, lodging, food – and a little about the history of the game. You will read about other things beyond golf that Scotland has to offer the Independent Golfer. Above all, you will read about 47 exceptional courses in the Highlands and Islands, where to find them, what they offer, and how to play them so that your time will be the most enjoyable possible.

So, Independent Golfer, read on and join those others of us who seek, whenever we can, to walk the magical fairways and greens of the Courses of the Highlands and Islands.

CHAPTER 2

Specially Designed by the Almighty for Playing Golf

Scotland is blessed with some of the most challenging, interesting, and famous courses in the world. Royal Troon, Glen Eagles, Turnberry, Muirfield, Loch Lomond, Carnoustie, and, of course, the Old Course at St. Andrews all bring to the American golfer's mind visions of rolling fairways, fast greens, and tightly fought British Open championships. Golf in Scotland is, for most of us, golf played on these championship courses. We all dream of one day following in the footsteps of Arnie and Jack when, arm in arm, they walked the final hole at St. Andrews to the cheers of thousands in the gallery, or to play across the Barry Burn to the 18th green at Carnoustie that bedeviled Jean Van de Velde in the 1999 British Open.

The challenge is that it is very difficult for most of us to play many of these courses. A number of the most famous Scottish courses are private, and thus limit play to members and their guests. Other courses are open to only limited public play, perhaps an afternoon or two per week. When you can get on them, they are overrun with other visitors who are traveling on company-financed tours or who have written months ahead or eve those who entered daily lotteries to secure tee times. Finally, because of their fame, most of these courses have become very expensive in recent years, often costing upwards of $200 for a round.

Golf is Scotland's game. There are hundreds of courses in this land of golf's birth that are owned by local groups of golfers or by municipalities, and thus by the people who live and work around the course. Golf in Scotland is very democratic.

Membership in most clubs is inexpensive, so much so that most avid Scottish golfers belong to two or three clubs at the same time. Elderly ladies come out together for nine holes in the summer evenings. Teenaged boys and girls play as a social activity. Men and women find time to escape from work to fit in a few holes at noon or before supper.

For most Scots, both the quality and the availability of their courses are of paramount importance. Most towns of any size sport a course that is lovingly maintained and supported by the locals just as it was enjoyed by the great-great-grand-parents of the current players. These courses are objects of pride for the community as well as an integral part of their social life.

To be sure, golf in Scotland, like most good things across the world, has suffered from population growth, urbanization, and the myriad distractions of modern life. In recent years, around the big cities of Glasgow and Edinburgh, numerous golf courses that are run as recreational businesses have been built. Urbanites flock there in search of a few hours of relief from city life and pay their green fees to play a round, much like their golfing counterparts do at the municipal and privately-owned-for-public-play courses across the U.S.A.

These newer courses around the Scottish cities' perimeters have a surprisingly similar feel to the good courses available for play in America. Their fairways are broad and tend to sweep slightly left or right, uphill or down. The rough is mown evenly in two or three stages, growing progressively deeper and more difficult as one drifts farther from the fairway. The greens are large, have gentle undulations that present a moderate level of challenge, and typically sport one or two shallow, green-side bunkers that add a bit of interest to the approach shot. All in all, these courses offer a surprisingly similar experience to what most Americans are accustomed to at home. But these courses are not what you will find in the Highlands and Islands. They probably shouldn't be included in the itinerary of the Independent Golfer. Why would you fly the Atlantic to play what you could play across town?

I don't want to imply that you should avoid playing some of Scotland's most famous golf courses. Of course, you need to play the Old Course at St. Andrews some time in your life. The sense of history and the challenge of the Old course, set as it is between the "auld grey toon" and the sea, is absolutely special.

But you should also know that, beyond the well-known courses on which the Opens are played and beyond the newer courses that ring Scotland's large cities, there is a wonderful world of Scottish golf that tends to be largely unknown to Americans. This is especially true across the grand and scenic Highlands and Islands of northern and western Scotland. Here are found a group of wonderfully rich courses, strung together like a necklace of sparkling gems in a curving arc from the Irish Sea in the West to the North Sea in the East. Each has its own character, and each is waiting to enchant the Independent Golfer who is willing to break away from the crowds, to take charge of his or her own golfing experience, and to venture off the well-trodden packaged tour paths.

These courses are set in wildly scenic landscapes, some along the links land by the sea, others nestled in the forested glens or by dark and lovely lochs (lakes) and rivers. Most are old, dating from the mid- to late- 1800's or, in some cases, even earlier. Many were designed by the original masters of Scottish golf like Old Tom Morris and James Braid and still bear the mark of men who thought that each hole on a course should present its own different challenge.

These are not driver-off-the-tee, short-iron, two-putt courses. They require you to think through options, to select your shot from a variety of options, to decide if the riskier shot is worth the greater reward. You might encounter a 520-yard par five that the wise golfer navigates with three good iron shots in order to work across a mountain stream to reach a saucer-shaped green protected by three deep bunkers. You might play a 265 yard par four that can take all the length you have in your driver, but only if you strike the ball on a line well to the left of the pin so that it rolls past an enormous fairway bunker and then curves with the contour of the fairway around toward your goal.

At each end of this necklace of gems, like magnificent jewels, lie two of the greatest golf courses in the world. In the southwest is Machrihanish on the tip of the Peninsula of Kintyre, lying within yards of the Irish Sea. Royal Dornoch is in the northeast above Inverness on the coast of the North Sea. Both of these are absolutely world-class golf courses that offer the Independent Golfer all that could possibly be asked for as a test of golf. Each is regularly ranked highly on various published lists of "the world's greatest courses." As an example, in its May 2005 issue, *Golf Magazine* ranked Royal Dornoch's Championship Course the fifth best course in the world outside the U.S.A., and the second best course in Scotland. In their editors' opinion, it was only bettered in Scotland by the Old Course at St. Andrews. In the same article, Machrihanish was ranked 39th best in the world and 10th best in Scotland.

Copeland 2006

Playing Royal Dornoch's Championship Course

Both of these gems are classic links courses. When Old Tom Morris declared in 1879 that the links at Machrihanish "…had been specially designed by the Almighty for playing golf," he was, of course, flattering his hosts on their newly created golf club. But he was also speaking truly of the grassy terrain between arable land and wild ocean on which these courses, and many others along Scotland's coasts, are located. Machrihanish and Royal Dornoch reward effective use of a wide variety of shots. Their length is demanding. Their greens are large, well maintained and putt truly. All who play them agree that the quality of golf they offer isn't bettered anyplace in the world.

As you play either of these marvelous jewels, you work your way along undulating fairways, avoiding deep bunkers that are cunningly placed where errant shots are likely to go. You may find yourself needing to hit a tee shot over an ancient dune now covered with grass to a blind landing area. You are always within a few yards of the ocean and continually feel the need to pause to take in wide and grand vistas of sea, mountain, dunes, and sky around you. You sense that you are playing golf where the greats of the past learned their sport and you are pleasantly humbled by the need to unlock the subtleties of the courses that they knew so well.

Another considerable attraction that these courses have for Independent Golfers is their cost. At the height of the summer season, you can play a weekday round on Royal Dornoch's Championship course, the 4th best golf course in the world outside of the United States, for £75.00 ($127.50)*. A comparable round on Machrihanish will cost you £40.00 ($68.00).

So, why have most Americans never heard of these two great courses? Certainly, every golfer who has played either of

---

* Throughout this book I will list prices of things where appropriate in order to give the reader a feeling for costs. These are approximate for two reasons. Like everywhere, prices in Scotland are rising. Those listed here were updated, wherever possible, to what you would have encountered in the Summer, 2006. Second, the conversion from British Pounds to American Dollars is dependent on money market rates that fluctuate daily. For the conversions that I list in this book, I used a rate of $1.70/£1.00.

them agrees that, as a place to play golf, they offer at least as much or perhaps even more than the more well-known courses on which the British Open is played. Why do Royal Dornoch and Machrihanish remain unknown to most Americans?

To stage successfully a world-class competition, promoters need more than a world-class golf course. They need access to hundreds of hotel rooms, acres of land to house the tent villages with their manufacturers' booths and vendors' stands, and convenient access to transportation systems that will bring thousands of spectators to the venue. Royal Dornoch and Machrihanish are remote from population centers, and neither has the tourist infrastructure that is necessary for hosting international competitions. Machrihanish, located at the far end of a long peninsula in the sparsely populated west of Scotland, is surrounded by farmlands and ocean. The nearest village of any size is Campbeltown, 15 miles away. The only accommodations near the course are three bed-and-breakfast houses and a small, old hotel that has been converted to apartments which can be rented by the week. Royal Dornoch is in the far northeast of Scotland, an hour north of Inverness, the country's most northern city. Though the village sports some very nice small hotels and guest houses, it could not house a tenth of the people who throng to big international competitions.

But remoteness and lack of a large tourist infrastructure are absolutely no problem for the Independent Golfer. The courses are there, in all their splendor. Lodging and meals of a very high standard are readily available for you, your family, and friends. Green fees are much more reasonable than those of the other, more well-known Scottish courses. Tee times are available without booking months in advance or paying commissions to brokers. Most importantly, on these courses you can immerse yourself in the Scottish golf experience, arriving at the course when you want, unencumbered by a swarm of other touring golfers. You can walk off the 18th tee and into the local clubhouse, or down the road to a pub for a relaxed lunch. You can play a second round in the afternoon if you like. You can share stories with local Scots who seem always eager to rehash the day's round or the last Ryder Cup competition.

But Machrihanish and Royal Dornoch are just the start. Eighty-six other hidden gems of golf are sprinkled between these two great courses across the Highlands and Islands of northern and western Scotland. Some of them are small and quaint, the only paid staff being the greens keeper who is out mowing the fairways when you arrive. In this case, before you play you are asked to deposit your green fee into a slot of an "honesty box" located in the modest clubhouse. Many are only nine-hole courses, but they are of such quality that they demand a second playing, or even a third. Some you might only decide to play if you are in the area for other reasons. But others in this string of gems offer a quality of play that rivals their more famous sisters. They deserve to be planned into the itinerary of any Independent Golfer who is traveling northern Scotland in search of unsurpassed golf. Though locally run and maintained primarily for the enjoyment of the region's residents, these courses are universally welcoming to visitors. Above all, they are challenging, imaginative and, in the highest judgment of the Scottish golfer, offer a "true test of golf."

In the Northeast, on the edge of the North Sea, you will find the Brora Golf Club. The layout of the 18 holes on this very old course has hardly changed since it was designed by the great James Braid. It is one of the finest examples of true links golf that you will find anywhere in Scotland, and it will cost you just £28 ($47.60) for a round or £35 ($59.50) for the day (add £5 ($8.50) on a weekend). Brora rambles over gently rising and falling links land next to the sea, out nine holes toward the north-east and then nine back to the small but well-appointed clubhouse. Rolling, undulating fairways, approaches to the greens that accept bumped and run balls, sweeping views of sea, rough of wispy grass and gorse bushes, winding burns (streams) of peat-colored water, mountains and sky uninterrupted by trees or buildings, this course has it all.

Copeland 2006

The author on the #13 Hole "Snake" at the Brora Golf Club

Brora is so traditional that livestock still graze on it. They help by keeping the rough somewhat eaten back, lending to the course's feeling of openness and helping the golfer find erratic balls. Electrical wires carrying a small direct current circle each green about 18 inches above the ground to keep the sheep off. A local rule reads that these electric fences "...should be treated as immovable obstructions. Relief should be taken in accordance with Rule 24-2. A ball striking any part of the fence may be replayed." Further, to be safe, another local rule states that, "Animal droppings on the course may be treated as casual water." This is more a curiosity than a problem. Don't be put off. The sheep and cows typically keep out of the way. (They learned long ago that they don't like electrical shocks.) The greens keeper turns the electricity off during the day, and most animal droppings are confined to the more remote parts of the course.

Down the coast near the city of Inverness, you will find the Fortrose and Rosemarkie Golf Club. This old links course, on

Copeland 2006

The Fortrose and Rosemarkie course, which straddles the Chanonry Ness near Inverness, starts at the clubhouse just beyond the village on the far left, extends out toward the lighthouse in the distance and then back down the right side of the road. The final holes again cross the road to end at the clubhouse.

which golf has been played since 1702, is dramatically situated on the Chanonry Ness, a long, thin peninsula that is only two fairways wide and thrusts out into the Moray Firth. You play with ocean on three sides, sometimes within mere yards of the tidelands, over links land spotted with heather, gorse, and a few low pines. The lighthouse at the end of the Ness is almost always in sight and beyond it, across the dark Firth, looms Fort George with its massive, sloping, canonball-proof walls that have been protecting the seaway access to Inverness since 1748. The course even boasts its own school of dolphins that can often be seen playing off of the first five fairways.

In Scotland's Western Highlands, just outside of the town of Inveraray on the shore of beautiful Loch Fyne you will find Inveraray Golf Club. Just a 9-hole, par 34 track, you will not play a more naturally beautiful course in your life. Drop your green fee of £15 ($25.50) into the slot in the small clubhouse's "honesty box" and play all day, as many rounds as you like. Though golf has been played in Inveraray for over 100 years, this course is new, having been built in 1993. The architect took maximum advantage of magnificent existing old-growth oak, birch, and beech trees to frame his greens and to create chutes out of which you drive your tee shots to broad, gently sloping fairways. Its #4 hole "Riochan" (the Scots name all their golf holes) offers a classic example of a "risk and reward" choice that is so characteristic of Scottish courses. It is only 355 yards but is complicated by a small burn that crosses the fairway about 217 yards in front of the tee. A drive of 235 yards can carry it. It is a bit downhill, which should help you. Do you lay up, leaving yourself 150 or more to the green, or do you go long, hoping for a short iron and a possible birdie?

North of Inveraray, around a ridge of pine-covered mountains, you will find Dragon's Tooth, another new 9-holer that was only opened in the Spring of 2002. Built by a family of farming folk on the banks of Loch Linnhe, this course expresses the family's pride of ownership and attention to detail in everything from its lush fairways and pristine greens (designed to European PGA standards) to its well-manicured foot-paths and tidy clubhouse that features freshly cut flowers on the dining tables. You can play a round for £10 ($17). Dragon Tooth's #8 "Down the Burn" is a short, slightly downhill, 474 par-5 that will both tempt your sense of adventure and tax your skills. A small burn runs in the trees down the right side the entire length of the hole. The green is tucked to the right around the corner at the end of the trees, across the burn. The normal, safe play is to hit your tee shot anywhere in the fairway and your second shot at the far right of the two great trees in the distance near the loch. This gives you a good angle and a short distance as you turn right, around the corner of the trees, to a green protected by a large bunker in the front left. However, if you feel bold and if your skills allow, you can reach the green in two. You must drive down the left (yes left) side of the fairway, always keeping

Courtesy Golf Highlands

Hole #3 "Twa Monkeys" at Dragon's Tooth Golf Course

out of the left rough, in order to have an angle to hit your second shot over the trees on the right and onto the green. Hitting into the left rough will cost you a stroke. An errant second shot will find the trees near the green and be even more costly. But two good shots can leave you putting for an eagle. Are you game to try?

These courses and others like them are set in some of the most scenic country you will ever encounter: islands floating in a dark green sea, narrow ocean inlets bounded by rocky shores below forested hills, fields of purple-blooming heather rolling up the sides of great, rounded mountains that were sculpted by ice-age glaciers. It is a land of narrow glens with small villages of stone, of seaside fishing towns, of green meadows with babbling streams and of rolling hills with patchwork fields dotted by sheep. This is the land of *Braveheart's* William Wallace and Robert Lewis Stevenson's Rob Roy MacGregor. Ruined medieval castles rise above trees on rocky outcrops. Quiet villages now sleep beside ancient battlefields on which the honor of clans or the succession of monarchies was contested. And amidst all of this are found the gem courses of the Highlands and Islands.

It is my aim in this book to open to American golfers the possibilities of golf in Scotland's Highlands and Islands. I suspect that most American golfers would jump at the opportunity to play golf as Scots play it, on some of the oldest and most intriguing courses in the world. They would thrill at the wild beauty of links golf played far from great crowds on layouts that challenge their game, not their pocketbook. They would prefer playing with locals, within sight of heather-covered mountains, rather than with tourists within sight of high-rise hotels. They would look forward to after-round conviviality in modest clubhouses and pubs with locals eager to talk the day's round through.

If I am right, and this "other" golf in Scotland, this non-touristized golf played by Scots on their own home courses, appeals to you, then you have to play golf in Scotland's north. Can you see yourself and perhaps a few close friends playing a course originally laid out by Old Tom Morris and enjoyed by generations of Scottish golfers that followed him? Do you relish play on courses that present a wide variety of challenges as they ask you to use every club in your bag? Would it be even more appealing if those courses were washed with the salty aromas of the nearby sea or set amid gently rolling, pine-covered hills? Would you appreciate paying $30 for a whole day of golf on a course that is as long on challenge as it is short on crowds? If this is what you would look for in a golf vacation to Scotland, then golf in the Highlands and Islands is for you.

CHAPTER 3

When in Scotland, Play As the Scots Play

American and Scottish golf aren't the same. I'm not talking about the rules that are, in fact, quite similar. The Royal and Ancient, which governs golf in most of the world, and the U.S. Golf Association, which rules our neck of the woods, have done a nice job of weeding out differences so that the rules, as the basis of the game, are similarly understood wherever one plays.

But the customs, traditions, and habits of play vary between America and Scotland in interesting ways. For a visitor to Scotland, especially for the Independent Golfer who is looking for a rich Scottish golfing experience, it pays to understand the subtleties of Scottish play, the meanings of words and phrases that Scots typically use, and the customs that govern their interactions on the course.

I know of a group from Iowa who had written the Secretary at Muirfield Golf Course to schedule a tee time. Muirfield, the home of the Honourable Company of Edinburgh Golfers and one of the courses in the British Open rota, is a wonderful seaside links course but has developed a notoriously inhospitable reputation. Visitors are only allowed on the course at limited times, green fees are quite steep, and stories are told of how Secretaries are less than inviting to non-member play. The Cornhuskers were delighted to receive a return letter that offered them the opportunity to play a foursome at 8:30 in the morning on a given date. When they arrived at the appointed time, however, they were told that, being a foursome, they would be limited to playing one ball per team of two, alternate shot. Each person could not hit his own ball!

To be fair, this is the common understanding in Scotland of the meaning of the term "foursome." Having a group of four players, each hitting his or her own ball, is called a "four-ball" there, not a "foursome." The Honorable Golfers of Muirfield apparently feel that limiting visitors to playing this alternate shot format reduces the non-member impact on their course. Such a limit on format is not common on most Scottish courses. Some, such as Royal Dornoch, might schedule only two-ball matches at certain times of the day to speed up play, but most courses are more than happy to let you play any format you wish.

When the folks from Iowa complained, they were politely but firmly told that, if they wanted to play a four-ball match, which is what they thought they had come to do, they "…might find that the little course down the road – Gullane – might be able to accommodate them."

Most who have played them agree that the experience of playing Gullane #1 certainly rivals that of playing Muirfield. Although it lacks the surrounding tourist infrastructure and persuasive lobbying by well-placed members that keeps Muirfield at the top of the list of courses holding international competitions, Gullane offers an outstanding links golf experience. The Iowa folks would not have been harmed by taking their clubs and going "down the road." But the point is that this small distinction between their understanding of the term "foursome" and that of the officials at Muirfield led to an unfortunate confusion and, for a short time at least, to some hard feelings.

In the pages that follow, I would like to share some thoughts about differences between play in Scotland and play with which most Americans are accustomed. In most cases, there is nothing "right or wrong" about these differences. They are just different. I do find that most visiting Americans are eager to follow the old adage, "When in Scotland, play as the Scots play." They just want to know how Scots play.

———

Links Golf.

For most people, the defining quality of golf in Scotland is that it is played on links courses. This is, of course, not completely true. There are many wonderful courses in the Highlands and Islands that are not links courses. But the links, that strip of ground with little agricultural value that stretches between the sea and the land and "links" the two, is where golf was first played. A links course is always selected to serve up the peculiarly Scottish challenge that is the British Open (even when it is played in England).

A few years ago, I played a course in Central California that was not only labeled a links-type course, but it also presumed to name itself The Links Course. After playing it and being decidedly disappointed (why should I have thought that I might have found a real links course in the farmland of California's Central Valley), I asked the resident pro why they called their course a links-type course. "It's windy and there are no trees," he smugly replied.

Courtesy Golf Highlands

The #6 green at Reay Golf Club illustrates the open, seaside nature of links golf. Reay is the most northerly 18-hole course on the British mainland. Sandside Bay and the Pentland Firth are in the background.

It is true that links courses typically have no trees. It is also true that they normally feature no great changes in elevation, that they tend to be built near the ocean, and that the wind often blows. But none of this gets to the central quality of the links course, which is the way it wants to be played.

Standing on the tee, a non-links player will look out to a target toward which he would like his ball to fly. The target will be someplace in a larger landing area into which he will be happy if his ball settles. The visual image he holds in his head of his tee shot is the arching trajectory of the ball through the air, defined at its near end by the tee box and at the far end by the patch of fairway where his ball should land. Similarly, as he addresses his approach shot, he sees the circle of green as his target. The center of the target might be the center of the green, or he might be tempted to narrow his target to be the pin or an area in the green from which a makeable putt can be stroked. Whatever the target, he intends that his ball will fly there and, if he is very skillful, stick in that spot (or perhaps even spin back a bit in the way that he sees the pros do on television).

The golfer who is sensitive to the qualities of the links course has a very different mental image as he stands on the tee. He thinks that the ground he is playing over is as important as the ground he is playing to. He is as concerned about the path his ball will follow as it rolls along the fairway as he is about its trajectory through the air. His visual image of his shot includes the intervening ground between himself and where he intends his ball to come to rest. He has less trust in the vagaries of a full 8-iron hit up into a stiff crosswind than he does in a medium swing put on a 5-iron that makes the ball hit 75 yards in front of the green with the expectation that it will bound toward the pin, twisting and rolling with the undulations of the fairway as it goes.

Why the difference? Golf on a links course must be understood as a system that perfectly integrates style of play with place. The place is a fortuitous combination of sandy soil, grasses and low foliage, weather, and topography that combine in just the right way to reward a specific style of play that has developed over the centuries. Its tight, wiry grasses centuries ago put down roots to stabilize drifting sand between the receding ocean and the more fertile farmland at a distance from the sea This grass now covers rolling, undulating fairways that have clear and telling effects on the ball's roll. So the golfer on a links course learns to look ahead to how his ball will roll as well as to how it will fly. Such accepting fairways would not be as important to the game if it weren't played in the normally windy conditions typical of seaside links courses. So the golfer on a links course learns to pay close attention to the wind, to go high to use it when possible and to go low to avoid it when necessary. The contours of links fairways would not be present if the land on which they lay were not, in an earlier incarnation, drifting dunes of sand that could only have developed along the seaside. So, although overall elevation change is never great on a links course, the links golfer learns to navigate cautiously through the knolls, hollows, and gullies of these ancient dunes, at times

Courtesy Golf Highlands

The 8th Hole "Delnies" at Nairn Golf Club offers the challenge of links golf at its best.

hitting blindly to greens just over the brow of a mound and at other times using the bank of the fairway to coax his ball to run around the turn of a dogleg as it rolls closer to the target.

The hardy grasses that offer such a perfect carpet for the bounce and roll of golf balls are kept healthy by the same wind-blown, salt-laden spray from winter storms that keeps other, less desirable grasses from establishing themselves near the sea. So the golfer on a links course is confident that a ball putted from off the green will roll well and true and not be deflected by thick clumps of "foreign" grasses that would interfere with a well-laid plan. Scots are firm in their belief that, from off the green, a poorly stroked putt will always give a better result than a poorly stroked pitch or chip.

These grasses, and the sandy seaside soils on which they grow, are keys to links golf. Cropped close, fescue grasses make wonderful fairways that encourage tee shots to roll well and present excellent lies from which irons can be struck. Left to grow, they become beige, wispy tracks of rough in which errant balls may be found but from which clean recovery shots are

Copeland 2006

A demonstration of the effects of animal grazing on links grasses on Handa Island.

almost impossible. The practice of mowing links courses is just over 100 years old. Modern greenskeepers adjust their mowers to replicate, as best they can, the conditions of fairways and roughs characteristic of the old links courses on which golf developed over the centuries. Before the mower was adopted as a greenskeeper's tool, courses depended on grazing animals – sheep, cattle and rabbits – to maintain their fairways in playable condition.

An interesting demonstration of the effects of the grazing of different animals on links grasses is depicted in the photograph at the left which, was taken on Handa Island on Scotland's north-west coast. A naturalist set up three controlled grazing conditions. The square defined by the central four posts is surrounded by a fine-mesh wire fence that excludes all grass-grazing animals. The grass inside it is left to grow to a natural height that corresponds to the deep rough, or "heavy", found on most links courses. The square on the left is surrounded by a very coarse-meshed wire fence. The openings are small enough to exclude sheep but large enough to admit rabbits. As you can see,

Copeland 2006

Sheep wallow showing the origin of bunkers on links land to the south of the Struie Course at Dornoch.

the rabbits have kept the grass somewhat short, a characteristic length of the light rough of links courses. The square on the right is defined simply by a rope that keeps people off but admits sheep as well as rabbits. You can see that their combined grazing efforts have cropped the grass down almost to modern fairway height. Here we see what the fairways of the 18th and 19th century Scottish links courses must have been like.

Animals have had their influence on the way that golf is played in other ways as well. In golf's early days, sheep that were turned out to graze on the links land had the habit of "wallowing down" into the grass and sandy soil in an effort to seek protection from the cold winds blowing in off the sea. Rather than seeing these resulting sheep wallows as intrusive interference into their enjoyment of the game, early golfers just took the animal-made obstacles as part of the game, tried to avoid hitting balls into them wherever possible, and developed techniques for hitting out when the inevitable finally happened. Thus, sand traps or bunkers were born.

These forces – the grasses, the rolling ancient dunes on which they grow, the nearby sea, the wind – all combine to encourage a style of play that must be more imaginative than that found on courses to which we Americans are accustomed. Links players are less likely to repeatedly put a full swing on each club. After a mighty swing put my tee shot in the left rough for the third hole in a row on the Tain Golf Club's course the grizzled old Scot with whom I was playing offered this observation as indirect advice: "Ye canna o'r power this course." Links players instead find themselves deciding whether to hit it full and high, punch it in low, or hit a half-swing bump-and-run with a lower-lofted club. Links players don't just pitch or chip at the pin. The undulations of aprons and greens call for careful thought as to how the ball will run on, curve, and hopefully roll toward the hole.

For some shots, links players will find themselves thinking carefully through a range of possibilities. Not all 380 yard holes call for a driver off the tee. A ball nestled down in the "heavy"

12 yards off the fairway and 140 yards from the green might better be chipped with a sand iron back into the fairway than be blasted with a 7-iron toward the distant green. Sitting 240 yards from the green after a drive on a par-5, the better shot might be a 7-iron that comes up short of a patch of thorny gorse that stretches across the left half of the fairway than a 3-wood that might fly to the right of the gorse, but might not.

In the final analysis, the links course wants to be played to its fullest. It asks you to consider options, to think about the wind and the roll of the fairway, to inventory your bag searching for just the shot that would have the best chance for success in the conditions you face. It wants to present you with choices and deal out rewards and consequences commensurate with the chances you take and the skill you employ. The links course wants to offer a complete test of the player. It wants you to thrill with the success of a good plan well executed, and it wants you to feel the pain of a bad choice or a poor swing. Above all, it wants you to experience both the challenge and the freedom of

Courtesy Golf Highlands

Looking across the gorse and broom toward the #17 green at Tain Golf Club.

playing golf as the founders of the game did, close to the sea and the elements with only their skill – and a wee bit of luck – to sustain them in their quest for a rewarding round.

And finally, there is the added bonus of playing this style of golf in the majestic openness offered by the links setting. On the good links course, the sky and its billowing clouds display the grand, all-encompassing sweep characteristic of the American West's Big-Sky country. The sea is always close by, either directly in view or just yards off over the hummocks and mounds of the links. The wind, light or strong, always brings a clean and exhilarating freshness. Views from the course's higher spots can be of expansive ocean, rocky shores, and rolling hills that shelter small towns from which distance has stripped their modernity, leaving a medieval heritage of stone fronts, steeply pitched roofs and church spires.

It is little wonder that Americans who know about links golf, who have experienced its challenge and exulted in the successes they have found, are willing to fly the Atlantic to get back to this game by the sea. We who have been there know the joy, the freedom, and, yes, the frustrations, of a game that, once played, can never be forgotten.

Other Styles of Scottish Golf

Not all Scottish golf is played on the links. In fact, of the eighty-eight courses currently found in the Highlands and Islands of Scotland, only 33 are actual links courses. Fifteen courses, labeled "Parkland", wander among beautifully manicured stands of old-growth deciduous trees, are kept in garden-like condition by dedicated groundskeepers and often feature babbling brooks, ponds and even water falls. Other courses, called "Inland", are laid out in rolling farmlands or meadows. "Heathland" courses are built inland but have soil that is similar to links land, which is typically more nutrient-poor, sandy, or peaty. These courses support more scrubby vegetation such as heather and gorse.

As to their style of play, parkland and inland courses are much closer to the feeling of a good American course than they are to links courses. They typically have a more manicured

Courtesy Golf Highlands

The Aigas Golf Course offers golf in a beautiful inland setting on the Beauly River near the entrance to Glen Afric. This is Hole #6 "Gorge."

appearance. The fairways can be broader and tend to feature more wide, sweeping curves and less angled doglegs than do links courses. The rough tends to be more uniform and may be cut in stages of increasing height as you move out from the fairway. Many are built along streams or lochs (lakes) or in valleys nestled among forest-covered hills. Overall elevation changes on some of these courses can be considerable.

As a result, play on these courses can be more similar to what Americans are accustomed to than the links course. Most of my friends who travel to Scotland look for the excitement and challenge of links play. But, after a few days of focused concentration and battle with the elements by the ocean, they are happy to take a "vacation" from the links to lapse into the old and familiar and relax at a good parkland or inland course. These courses offer a delightful variation, often in magnificent mountain settings, and should be included in any well-rounded golf itinerary in the Highlands and Islands.

The Importance of Competition

I was by myself one afternoon on the putting green near the first tee at Royal Dornoch' Championship Course when a fellow walked up and asked if I would like to play a round. With no other golfers present to slow our play and with only a light breeze coming in from the ocean, I eagerly accepted his invitation. We introduced ourselves, I a visitor from America and he a "country member" of Royal Dornoch. David didn't reside in or near the village of Dornoch. He was a separated Scotsman, married to an English woman and living near Birmingham. He was retired and came north five or six times a year because he could find no better place to play golf than the links at Dornoch. His "country membership" gave him full privileges on the course.

As we loosened up on the first tee, he asked, "What da ye play off a?" This is a very common question among Scottish golfers. Scots are generally hesitant to ask personal questions. Your marital status, the kind of work you do, or the number of children you have does not easily come up in conversation, unless raised by Americans who always seem to be more willing to ask such personal questions than are Scots. But for Scottish golfers, your handicap – what you play off of – is a vital piece of information that they need to know at the earliest opportunity.

I explained that I didn't have a Scottish Golf Union handicap but that my US Golf Association index was a 7.4 and that I reckoned my handicap on Royal Dornoch might be about 9 or 10. He volunteered that he played off a 6.

He then smiled and asked, "Would you fancy a wee competition?" Uh, oh, I thought. Here this guy is, not knowing me for five minutes and already wanting to get into my pocket. But before I could fashion an appropriate response, he clarified, "We needn't play for anything, jus' for the honor o' the game. What da ye say?"

Well, I agreed and we were off, playing a match-play game in the great tradition of Scottish golf. Scots love to compete. While Americans are accustomed to perhaps monthly club events, a yearly club championship, and perhaps an occasional charity event, in Scotland competitions are always going on. Through the year almost every club in Scotland will hold an "open", which any golfer with an established handicap can enter. In addition to yearly club championship tournaments, clubs conduct on-going match-play competitions in which individual matches are scheduled by the players to be completed by given dates. To give you an idea of the amount of competition found in the Highlands and Islands, between March and October of 2005 in the area around Inverness and the north-east Highlands alone, almost 350 separate competitions were held, including 171 for men, 64 for women, 28 for seniors, 44 "mixed", and 37 for juniors. It is inevitable that, when Scots get together to play, they declare a "competition" and have at it.

Three American friends of mine and I were invited to play a round with four Scots at the Nairn Golf Club, a championship-quality course sited on the links land near the Morray Firth, just a few miles east of Inverness. Half-way between the clubhouse and the first tee, one of the Scots raised the possibility of a friendly match. By the time our first group was ready to tee off, the format was decided, competing teams designated, and our match had been declared a mini-Ryder Cup!

The interesting thing about these informal competitions is that stakes don't matter. My Dornoch friend, David, was happy to play for just the honor of the game. Our Nairn hosts were not interested in specifying what we were playing for, just that we were competing. It turned out that David and I played nearly even, enjoyed our time together, and agreed to play again a few days later. When we came together on the 1st tee for our 2nd match, eager to "play as the Scots play" I volunteered that we have another match and that this time we should at least play for a pint to be collected in the clubhouse after. David was delighted to agree, and I eventually paid. But it was clear that winning the beer was not important to him. Playing the match was.

There is good logic in this. Conditions on Scottish courses, especially links courses, can change radically from day to day and, many times, from hour to hour in a given day. This makes the concept of par relatively insignificant. Shooting par on a 435 yard par-4 hole on a sunny, calm day may be difficult, but on the next day, with a 35 mile per hour wind blowing rain in your face, it becomes impossible. "Par" in fact, is only an expression of distance. It is simply the sum of the number of strokes a golfer should normally need to cover the distance from tee to green – one, two or three – plus two strokes for putting. But the wind blowing from behind can make reaching a 495 yard par-5 in two strokes easy while, on the next hole, the same wind can make reaching a 205 yard par-3 in one stroke impossible.

Some Scottish friends and I had just completed an exhilarating match under blue sky and white clouds at Kingussie Golf Club, a wonderful inland course built over 100 years ago set in sloping hills that edge down into the valley of the River Spey. As we enjoyed a post-match round of drinks in the comfortable Kingussie clubhouse this subject of competition and par came up. Norman Macwilliam, one of our group, had firmly-held opinions on the issue, and you would be well-advised to pay attention to Norman's views on golf. He is a Past-Secretary of the Kingussie Golf Club, having served in that capacity for many years. But more, Norman has won the Club Championship of Kingussie a remarkable thirteen times, a feat seldom achieved by any golfer at any club in the Highlands and Islands. Finally, Norman also holds the Kingussie course record of 7 under par 60, his scorecard still prominently displayed in the clubhouse's trophy case. When the conversation is about golf, Norman knows what he is talking about.

We often hear that a virtue of the game of golf is that "you are competing against yourself." It is true that, psychological issues aside, there is nothing that one competitor in a golf match can do to influence the play of another competitor. But, given the changing conditions typical of a day on a Scottish course, Norman maintains that it is difficult to gauge how well you are playing if you only measure yourself against par. A three on a short par-3 buffeted by a vicious cross wind is not just reasonably good play, it is a major victory, as is a five on a long par-4 played up hill against the wind.

Norman suggests that the best measure of your play on any given day is to compare it not to par but to the play of another who is playing right along beside you, facing the same weather conditions and feeling the same pressures. Norman goes so far as to suggest that the whole idea of par might be "redundant." (Redundant is a label used in Great Britain for anything that has lost its usefulness. Scotland has many old church buildings that, as attendance dwindled in recent years, have been declared redundant and were closed to save money. Workers whose jobs become unnecessary to the company because of automation or outsourcing are declared "redundant" and are let go.) For Norman, the idea of "par" has very little usefulness. I think that is why Scot golfers are always so eager to whomp up a friendly, match, even with strangers and nothing on the line. They are not so much competing against each other as they are setting up a way to measure their own play, not against par but against an outside index that is sensitive to the conditions of play on that day.

The kind of game that Scots prefer is interesting, too. On a Scottish course, you seldom hear of "greenies,",\ "specks," "choose 'ems," "skins," "wolf," "double for a birdie," "press," or most of the other devices that Americans have dreamt up over the years as ways to exchange money on the course. Scots love match play, one player against another, one hole at a time. For them, there is no need to record one player's 4 to another's 7 on a hole. Total strokes signify little. The first player simply won the hole. The score card shows that he is one-up. That is all that is necessary.

There are, of course, variations. Four players may compete in Scottish Four-ball where two teams of two players compete, with each player playing his own ball. If a player scores less than either of the players on the other team, his team wins the hole. In Scotland, playing a "foursome" is strictly a two-ball match with two players on a team alternating shots. But here again, the essence is match play. The lower score wins the hole, and winning the hole is all that counts.

Warming Up

Most Americans are accustomed to going to the range and hitting a bucket of balls before play. We see the PGA pros all doing this, and we think it is good for us as well. I must admit that I feel more awkward than usual on the first tee if I haven't had the opportunity to club a few balls on the range first.

The Scots apparently don't have this need. How do we know? Because most courses just don't have driving ranges. It is very common to see a few locals arrive in the car park, go into the clubhouse to change shoes, and then go directly to the first tee to start their match. No swinging of clubs or even stretching here. Just arrive and go.

Apparently the Scots are aware that they have a reputation for not having ranges associated with their courses. In the 2005 issue of *The Official Guide to Golf in Scotland,* the publishers write that the "myth" that Scotland has limited practice facilities should be "exploded". As evidence, they point out that there are "...over 60 superb practice facilities all open to visitors in Scotland...." Hey guys, sixty facilities in a country with 546 golf courses? That's hardly evidence of a commitment to warming up before a match!

If, as I do, you need time to swing the club before venturing out, you will find that many courses have one or two small cages hung with nets into which you can hit balls off of artificial-turf practice mats. You can't track the ball flight, but you can work on your timing and get a feel for the day. It is better than nothing.

Time of Play.

Scots do not dally when they play their golf. From their opening stroke on the first tee to the last putt on 18, they play with an unerring determination to get to the ball, hit it, and move on. I do not mean to imply that there is anything hasty about Scots' play. They commonly take the time necessary to go though a reasonable pre-shot routine, to line up a putt, or to make a short conversational comment on the flight of a ball or the break of the green. But golf is what they are out there to play, and play it they will.

We Americans have a reputation in Scotland, deservedly or not, for slow play. The story is told of one of the venerable caddies at Royal Dornoch, Alexander Matheson, and the day he looped for two visiting Americans. Alexander, known to everybody by his nickname "Pipey", was carrying both clients' bags that day as they started play at 11:00 in the morning. The day was apparently filled with lost balls, conversations among the clients about what went wrong, long bouts of waggling over tee shots, slow walks from tee to ball, repeated consultations about the potential break of putts, all interrupted by exclamations about and pauses to appreciate the beautiful scenic views of the Sutherland coast on which they were playing. As Pipey lugged the two bags up to the 18th green at 4:00 in the afternoon, five hours after they had started, one of the clients noticed a hint of fatigue on his face and sympathetically remarked, "Pipey, you look a little tired." Without hesitation, Pipey's retort came back, "A'm noo so much tiret as haimsick."

Five hours is exceptionally long for a round anyplace, but Scots think that 4 1/2 would be entirely too long as well. They would like a group of four to finish under four hours and a group of two under three and one half.

The push for faster play that we experience on American public courses derives largely from the course's desire to move as many paying customers as is possible through 18 holes in the day. This may also be the case at the more famous and heavily-played courses in Scotland, but on many of the courses in the Highlands and Islands, the number of people playing is small, and it is quite uncommon for groups to be backed up waiting for the next group to clear the green ahead. Yet, a brisk pace of play is still important. Scots might laugh and say it is the lure of the pint of lager or dram of whiskey to be had in the clubhouse after the round that moves them about the course but, in fact, they are simply accustomed to a pace of play different from golf in America. Why? I suspect this is the product of a combination of things.

Underlying it all is a sense of what a round on the course should be. For Scots, it is primarily to play golf. Conversation is common, but it is secondary to the game and is therefore brief and never interferes with play. Scots wonder about our tendency to stand and talk after exiting a green and before moving to the next tee.

Other things not directly related to the game are much less common on Scottish courses compared to those in America. Scots shake their heads at our desire to take a picnic onto the course with us. Why would you want to play golf with a sandwich, beer, and pretzels in your hands? Their prototypical view of an American golfer is a fellow lounging in a buggy (an electric cart) with a hotdog in hand and a beer in the holder below the steering wheel. Scots, of course, are no strangers to beer and sandwiches, but they prefer to indulge after the round, in the clubhouse. There they will talk, laugh, drink, and eat for as long as any American would like. Such companionship is, in fact, as much a part of the golf experience for Scots as is the time on the course. But the time on the course is for golf, not for activities that they feel belong in the clubhouse.

The use of electric carts (buggies) is another factor that slows down play for Americans. The club pros in America, who typically own the electric cart concessions on their courses, have convinced us that an electric cart should be as common a piece of equipment on the course as a 7-iron. Courses are designed for cart use: cement cart paths line the fairways, distances between greens and next tees are long. As a consequence, American golfers have, by and large, bought into the belief that one must ride, not walk, the course. However, the result is slow play.

It is common in our country to see a pair ride to a golfer's ball where one fellow climbs out of the cart, selects a club, looks out at his target, goes through his pre-shot routine, and hits. All the time his partner lounges in the cart nearby and watches. The first golfer then gets back in, and they turn to ride across the fairway to the second golfer's ball, where she disembarks, goes through the same process, and hits while her partner sits and watches. Neither walked more than six feet between rides. How much faster would play be if both had walked directly to their balls and made ready to swing when it was their turn?

Further, on many courses, carts are restricted to paths on the sides of fairways. You often see a golfer park the cart and walk, carrying a selected iron, into the fairway toward the ball, only to find that the distance to the green, that had been estimated from the side is wrong. The golfer must return to the cart for a different club, slowing play in the process.

I am a walker and must admit that such "cart play" bothers me, even in America. So I am happy to report that play slowed by "buggies" is not a problem in Scotland, where they are rarely seen. Most courses own one or two but, to use one, a golfer must produce a letter from a physician attesting to a medical condition that requires the golfer to use a buggy when playing.

There are signs that this limitation on buggy use is changing. A growing number of courses seem to be purchasing a few buggies in the hopes of attracting American golfers who want to play courses that allow them to ride as they play. Apparently, the management is willing to slow play in order to gain the increased revenues that buggy rental would bring. Such managers face the fact, however, that the layout of most Scottish courses makes buggy use fairly cumbersome. The mapping of holes, the locations of tees and greens, and the natural landforms and obstacles that range along fairways of the older courses were all developed for the walking golfer. Riders must often weave their way through the course and park at a distance from where they wish to play their ball. Who knows if we will see increased buggy use in the future in Scottish courses? As of now, walking is still the mode for play.

The style of competition preferred by Scots also contributes to brisk play. When golfers are engaged in a match-play competition and total strokes don't matter, it is common to concede putts instead of holing them out. You often hear a Scot golfer exclaim "Put it in your pocket" after his opponent has chipped her third shot to within 14 inches, especially if he is lying five at the time. Why play out if the outcome, who will win the hole, is not in doubt? This even extends to matches. I have seen local members walk in from the 17th hole at the Old Course and St. Andrews after a match was decided on the 16th green, leaving the last holes unplayed. Why play those last two holes if you are three down? Of course, this might not have been the action of visitors who had written 18 months earlier to secure a tee time and then paid the $190 green fee for non-members. But the point is made. The style of competition that Scots love tends to speed their game.

To be fair, Americans should not be faulted for wanting to putt out on every hole. We are accustomed to putting out because we are required to do so. Scots don't understand a critical difference between their handicap system and ours. The US Golf Association and its regional affiliates' rules require that we post <u>all</u> our scores. This is so important that the rules allow a club secretary to penalize a golfer who fails to post a score by adding an additional score to his or her record, that being the equivalent of the golfer's best score in her or his last twenty rounds. Our computer/internet system makes it easy to accumulate scores at both home and away courses. Our slope system allows us to compare these scores on different courses and to compute a personal handicap that is intended to reflect our current level of play. As a result, strokes can be fairly given and taken and competitions evened out among players with differing abilities. If we do not post all of our scores, the system cannot compute an accurate reflection of our current level of play. And we can't post our scores if we don't putt out or if we pick up after the 16th when down three. (Strictly speaking, the USGA handicap system offers ways to do this by estimating scores on holes not played, but most American golfers don't need these rules because they just play the last holes.)

The stroke handicap system is, in some ways, simpler in Scotland. For normal friendly matches, Scots are not required to submit their scores at all. Thus, conceded holes do not complicate the computation of one's handicap. Instead, handicaps are kept current by submitting only scores made during matches that are official competitions, when all strokes are taken and counted. Scots are required to submit a minimum of only three such scores a year in order to retain their handicap. As you might guess, because of their love of competition, most Scots submit many more scores than three.

Over the year, Scots typically submit fewer scores to their handicap system than do Americans. They feel that the scores that are submitted are more likely to be indicative of the player's true level of play. First of all, these scores were achieved under competitive circumstances when the pressure the player experienced might be heightened, and also when it is more likely that all the rules of golf will be meticulously observed. Further, under competitive conditions, Scots are tighter with their score-submitting process. During competitions, players must keep each other's scores, and the scorecards they submit must be attested to by the opponent's signature.

While all the above factors may contribute to differences in the pace of play between Scotland and America, I suspect that habit is the most telling factor of them all. Most Americans play their golf on public courses, and most public courses, especially the good ones, tend to be crowded places, especially on weekends. Play under these conditions is slow. We have grown accustomed to playing at a pace that is subconsciously calculated to reduce our waiting time on the next tee. Without being aware of it, we fit our pace of play into the flow of the others around the course. Not surprisingly, when the course is less crowded, we still fall into our habituated pace of play and finish only slightly faster than we would on more crowded days.

Most of the courses in the Highlands and Islands of Scotland are much less crowded. In all but the most famous

Courtesy Golf Highlands

Dornoch's Struie course with the Royal Burgh of Dornoch, dominated by its 780 year old cathedral, in the background.

courses, it is not uncommon to play with the nearest group three holes ahead or two holes behind you. Under these conditions, Scots have been able to develop a habit of more rapid play. Like ours, the habit tends to carry on, even onto more populated courses, so that play under any conditions, even more crowded ones, proceeds a bit faster.

"Playing through" is a much more common phenomenon in Scotland than in America. Because groups tend to be spaced much more widely around a Scottish course, when one group does overtake another, especially because of delays such as lost balls or simply beginner's play, the overtaken group commonly steps aside and extends the courtesy of allowing the faster group to play through rather than holding up their play. Being on an uncrowded course, the faster group can continue on playing at their pace, and the overtaken group can resume play with no lasting delay. As a result, inviting groups to "play through" is a much more common occurrence on Scottish courses than on American. And play proceeds a bit faster because of it.

For all this, play is more rapid in Scotland than we Americans are accustomed to. But if you agree to forego your refreshment until after the last putt on 18, if you get into the spirit of match play competition, if you follow all the common courtesies that all golfers know and should emulate – get to your ball promptly, be ready to hit when it is your turn – then you may find that this brisker rate of play invigorates your game and keeps your attention focused on the task at hand, getting that ball into the hole.

Dress

My buddy Orin wears shorts all the time, everywhere, for all reasons, in all seasons. If they would let him, I am sure that he would wear shorts on the flight deck of the jet that he flies for a large American airline. On a golfing trip to Scotland a few years ago, Orin predictably brought sufficient changes of shorts to see him through the two weeks we would be playing. I think he had one pair of long pants. Not only were the shorts comfortable for him, but they also allowed him to brag about how, as an experienced world traveler, he was able to get along with such a small suitcase while the others of us struggled with our bags packed with two weeks of long pants.

But Orin met his match on Elie, a beautiful seaside links course in Fife, on the north coast of the Firth of Forth. As we prepared to tee off, the starter informed Orin that shorts, as he was wearing them, were not permitted on the course. Elie presents a substantial test of golf in a beautiful setting (which at times wanders behind the village and at other times dips down to within yards of the sea). It is distinguished by its use of a periscope scavenged from a World War II submarine to look over a hill to determine if the players on the first fairway hit their second shots and have moved on so that those on the tee can begin. Elie is a serious course, but Orin did not think it would be so "stuffy" as to stop him from playing in shorts. Of course, the folks at Elie don't see it as "stuffy" but rather as a nod to order, stability, and decorum befitting the ancient game.

The Starter had a solution. Rather than prohibiting Orin from playing or making him drive 20 miles back to our Bed and Breakfast to retrieve his long pants, the Starter noted that one could wear shorts if one also wore long socks that reached the knee. Orin ducked into the pro shop and bought the only long socks they had, a cheap pair of gaudy, light-green beauties that clashed horribly with his blue Bermudas. Apparently, the local Elie rules don't require that a golfer be color conscious. Long socks of any hue were acceptable; the Starter was happy, and off we went on our round. The only downside to this whole experience was Nick's insistence that Orin stand behind him on the greens so as not to be a distraction while he putted.

Scots are not as formal as they were a few years ago, but many of the larger and more famous courses do have dress codes that the Independent Golfer should be aware of. Typically, wearing athletic shorts or warm-ups on the course is frowned upon. If shorts are to be worn, they should be long enough to reach almost to the knees, and they should be paired with knee socks. Shirts should have collars. Many courses still maintain a stricter dress code for the public rooms in their clubhouses, especially the dining room and the bar. Here they may require long pants, jackets, and ties. One never, at any course, wears golf shoes into these public rooms. Further, most courses would appreciate it if you not change your shoes in the parking lot. This is why carrying your shoes to the course in a bag and changing them in the locker room before and after play is a good idea. Your daily fee includes access to the locker room, and it is a good idea to use it.

Courtesy and Customs

Orin had just scrambled for his par after having hit his tee shot short and left on #3–"Drimnin," and he was happy. Ben had scored another par, his third in as many holes. He was happy, too. Nick and I shared the mood with our buddies, satisfied with our bogies on this difficult 230 yard par-3. We were playing a very interesting course that we had been looking forward to for some time. Tobermory is on the Isle of Mull on the west coast of Scotland, one of the real hidden "gems" of the Highlands and Islands. The Tobermory clubhouse proudly displays photos of Tom Watson with some local players, taken when Tom came to play this rather remarkable track that plays as a links-type course, though it is actually perched in the hills behind the seaside town from which it takes its name.

The day had started out quite well for us. Little wonder that we four were chattering, laughing, and generally exulting in each other's play as we walked from the third green onto the fourth tee. As Ben teed his ball and Orin made us snicker with his comment about how easy this golf game really is, Nick whispered rather loudly, "Guys, hold it down." I looked over to see, standing on the #6 tee but just a few feet away, four Scots waiting for us to play. They stood facing us in a posed row, equally spaced, each with folded arms and weight on his right foot, the other foot pushed out slightly to the front and left. The message was clear. They had arrived on their tee first but were now waiting for us, engaged in our loud revelry, to hit our tee shots. Struck silent, we managed embarrassed waves, gesturing for them to proceed. No, no. They were fine. We should go ahead, they said. Self-consciously and silently, we hit and skulked away.

This was a clear case in which some golfers' well-intended but nevertheless rather loud exuberation impinged on the enjoyment of others. To be sure, we weren't helped by the very close proximity of the #3 green to the #4 and #6 tees on Tobermory. We hadn't played the course before and didn't expect to see another tee so close to the one we were using. But this is common on many of the older courses in Scotland. Built decades or even centuries ago for gentlemen golfers to walk, teeing grounds on these courses are often just next to greens. Teeing grounds can be used for two different holes and, as we all know, it is not uncommon (even on the great courses like The Old Course at St. Andrews) to have two holes on a single green. A beauty of many links courses is that, though holes may, of necessity, be relatively close to each other, they are commonly separated by low hummocks, hills, and swales, giving you a feeling of being alone on your hole under the great sweep of sky. But your secluded feeling can be jarred as you walk over a small rise and encounter another group of golfers just a few yards away playing their shots. In these situations, courtesy needs to include a bit of quiet.

I need to be careful here because what it means to be "courteous" is very cultural. Americans are certainly very courteous and at their best when complimenting others for a job well done. We can't let a good stroke go by without making a comment. "Smooth swing!" "You really got into that one." Scots are equally courteous. "Brilliant" or "Ah. Well done" seems to follow every shot that isn't a total disaster.

The issue is how such courteous compliments are expressed. Americans have been raised to cheer loudly. Our sports teams have squads of specially-designated cheerleaders whose only job is to exhort us to ever-higher volume as we cheer our athletes on. A great tradition in our national pastime is to shout

This beautiful par-3 at Fort William Golf Club is complicated by a burn that surrounds the green on three sides - left, front and right - and a two-tiered green.

encouragement to our guy at the plate or on the mound. Our voices go up as our excitement and enthusiasm mounts.

By contrast, it is quite uncommon to hear Scots shout anything on a golf course. They are as inclined to praise and commendation as anybody, but it is given quietly, in a sincere but reserved way. When shouts of "All right," "Way to go," or "Yee ha" come drifting up the valley or across the grass-covered hills, it is a safe bet that it was an American who just sank a putt.

Golf, Scotland's national game, seems to be in the blood of most Scots. Nowhere is this more evident than in the ways that they display courteous behavior on the course. Not allowing enthusiasm to affect others' play is one thing. Also, allowing faster groups to play through is quite common. Scots are quick to compliment you on your play but they never make comments or offer suggestions as to how fellow golfers might improve their game.

A few other simple customs might be important to note as well. It is common for Scots to exchange a word or two of encouragement on the first tee before the round begins. Just a little "Play well today" or "Hit 'em straight" is all that is needed, but it does seem to start the day off on a courteous note.

Similarly, at the end of the round, the customary handshake and "Well played" is accompanied by a doffing of the cap. It's a small thing, but it is so very common in Scotland that a visitor almost feels like he is "living up to expectations" when he lifts his lid to his companions.

Courtesy even extends to non-players. It is very common to see non-playing Scots, alone or in pairs, walking along the edge of a course in the morning or evening. They often bring along their dogs to enjoy the outing. These walkers seem to get pleasure from watching golfers play but are very careful not to interfere with the game. They will stop their stroll at seemingly great distances from a player and stand quietly until the player has hit. It is not uncommon to see people stop 75 or even 100 yards away, well outside of any range from which they could possibly interfere, and wait patiently for the play to be made.

Distance Markers on the Course.

The U.S. Golf Association and its regional subsidiaries have gone a long way toward "standardizing" the game in America. True, the variation among golf courses in the U.S. is great, as it should be. Some courses are flat, wide open, and easy; others are hilly, narrow, tree-lined, and difficult. But, because of the Association's efforts, they all have some things in common. First, there are yardage markers on every hole that indicate distances to the center of the green: 100, 150, 200 and, where needed, 250 yards. Second, there is generally some system by which a golfer approaching a green can tell from a distance where the flag is located: front, center, or back. Third, there are officially-designated teeing areas for the average male and female golfers and also for golfers who have, or think they have, the ability to play long. Some courses even have teeing areas that make holes play very long, these for golfers who have very special abilities or who really like to punish themselves.

The reason for these course markings, in the American mind, is to even the playing field and reduce the home-course advantage by reducing the value of "local knowledge." When visitors come to an American course for a friendly competition, they don't need to know that the distance from the large oak on the left to the front of the green is 135 yards. They can pace off their ball's location from the 150 yard disk in the middle of the fairway.

As you might expect, this is all different in Scotland. First, many courses do not have any distance markers at all. Other courses do have distances marked off, but the systems used for this marking vary greatly from course to course. For example, the Aigas Golf Course near Inverness uses yellow disks placed in the center of the fairway, 150 yards from the center of each green. On the Fort William Golf Club course, a white stake for 200 yards and a yellow pipe for 150 yards, both at the side of the fairway, indicate distances from the green. Blue and red disk distance markers are placed in the fairway 125 and 175 yards, respectively, from the center of each green on the Fortrose and

Rosemarkie Golf Club course on the Black Isle. Some courses use markers in the fairway to indicate distances to the front of their greens, not to the center. Kings Acre south of Edinburgh places brightly-colored distance markers on each fairway, but at different distances from the green on each hole. On hole #1, the blue marker is 145 yards from the green, while on Hole #2 it is only 125 yards away. On this course, you must purchase a booklet in the pro shop with the markers' distances on each hole.

Second, on most Scottish courses, the pin is just cut where it is, with no prior indication that might help the approaching golfer. On links courses, which typically have nine holes running out along the sea coast and nine returning to the clubhouse, the clever Scot will note the pin placements of the return nine on the way out. Beyond that, you are simply on your own to seek the pin where you find it.

All Scottish courses do have designated lengths for their holes. The longest are the "medal tees" which are for competitions. The men's tees are a bit shorter, followed by the ladies', and finally the tees for juniors. These distances are normally written on the sides of small boxes used to designate one corner of the rectangular teeing area for the day. The difficulty is that the teeing areas, and thus the location of the boxes, change each day, but the designated distances painted on the boxes remain the same. The result is that the printed hole distances are only an approximation of what you will be playing on any day. On only a few Scottish courses do you find a distance marker on the tee that is anchored in the ground, offering a dependable yardage distance from it to the hole.

When we play Scottish courses, Americans find this lack of assistance with distances difficult for a couple of reasons. First, and most obviously, we aren't used to it. Always playing with distance markers available, we seldom practice seeing distances. Unless we have driven a ball wildly into an adjacent fairway, we are accustomed to locating the nearest marker disk or marked sprinkler head and pacing off the distance up or back to our ball. We peer ahead to the pin for direction, but use the yardage we have paced off to select our club.

Second, distances are deceiving in Scotland, especially on links courses. On these wonderfully varying tracks, it is seldom that you see an uninterrupted sweep of fairway running directly from your location up to the green. More likely, the fairway will have dips and hollows, crowns and hills. The green might be raised so that the flag is silhouetted against the sky or sunken so that you only see the top of the flag, or nothing at all. All of this tends to interfere with your depth perception, and makes judging distances difficult.

When asked why players in Scotland are given such little assistance with distances, Scots remark that golf should be played with the eye and with a feel for the game, not with yardage distances and a mental calculator. They think that a good golfer should be able to look out at the hole, see the distance, pick the club, and trust. Though to the American ear, this may sound a little harsh and unyielding, there may, in fact, be some justification for their position, and that justification gets back to links play. Given the generous distance that a ball can roll on a links fairway and the potential effects of wind on the flight of the ball near the sea, links golfers quite often strike balls with less than full swings. A three-quarter swing put on a five iron that sends the ball bounding down the fairway might yield much better results than a full seven iron that sends the ball higher into the wind. In these conditions, knowing the exact yardage that a shot must fly becomes much less important than considering the wind, the terrain, and the trajectory your shot must optimally follow to get to the green. Developing this "feel" for distance may be one of the most difficult tasks facing the American golfer in Scotland, but it also may be one of the most valuable abilities that you could bring back from a golfing holiday in the Highlands.

There is one other thing that should be said about tee markers in Scotland, and that is the sanctity of the competition tees. In America, any golfers who feel that they have the skill to play the course over the longer distance may use the back tees. While many of us should probably play the forward men's tees instead of the backs, it is up to us to decide.

Not so in Scotland. The rear tees, termed the "medal" or "competition tees," are reserved for contests, i.e., tournaments and set matches that are part of sanctioned competitions among members or between clubs. Scots do not want their competition tees torn up by daily casual play. They prefer to keep these tees pristine and ready for use by competitors in sanctioned matches.

This is a concept that is foreign to most Americans. When told that he cannot "play from the tips", an American golfer who believes he is a skillful player is likely to feel insulted. "What does the starter think, that I'm not good enough to play from the back tees?" He fails to notice that all the locals, visitors and members alike, are playing from the regular men's tees no matter their ability. Playing from the regular tees in Scotland is no reflection on your ability. Rather, it is a way to respect the high value that Scots place on competitive golf and their need to preserve the back teeing ground for competitions.

A Gentle Guide to Play

All of the above is not intended to make it seem that playing golf in Scotland is difficult. To the contrary, Scot golfers are among the most friendly and easy people to play with that you could hope to encounter. Their appreciation of the game leads to a respect for others who play and contributes to a natural camaraderie among devotees of the game.

Our similarities are great and differences small. It is my belief that most Americans, especially those traveling independently, are eager to respect local differences, to "fit in" and to join their Scottish playing partners in enjoying the game that they all love.

CHAPTER 4

Do Ye Ha a Time?

The word most Americans hear is that scheduling tee times on Scottish courses is "difficult." This is true only if you aim to play the well-known courses frequented by American golfers who are not aware of the wide range of excellent courses scattered across the Highlands and Islands. The St. Andrews Golf Trust recommends that you write to them 18 months ahead of time to get a start time on the Old Course. Royal Troon only accepts visitors three days a week, and during limited times on those days. Likewise, Muirfield only allows visitors onto their links on selected days of the week. Gleneagles and Turnberry give preference for tee times to those who stay at their resort hotels, an expensive condition to meet.

But for the Independent Golfer who plays the Highlands and Islands, the booking picture is much less limiting. My buddies and I had lingered a bit too long over lunch in the clubhouse after a morning round on Nairn. The good food, the comfortable clubhouse, and the interesting conversation with a couple of local characters we had met on the putting green all combined to make us extend our lunch well into the afternoon. We had planned to spend the afternoon on a tour of the Glenmorangie whiskey distillery but finally arrived there at 3:30, 30 minutes after the last tour began. A phone call ahead would have alerted us to their schedule, but we hadn't called, and we were stuck with nothing to do for the afternoon.

The young lady in the distillery visitor center was kind enough to "pour us a dram" of some of Glenmorangie's offerings. As we sipped samples, trying to determine the

Courtesy Golf Highlands

A most interesting bunker on the #9 Hole "Mafeking" at the Tain Golf Club

difference between their single malt aged in port oak barrels vs. that aged in Madeira oak barrels, Nick recalled that the Tain Golf Club course was just down the coast. "Let's go play a round at Tain!" As true Independent Golfers, we had no schedule to keep and no responsibilities to meet the remainder of that day other than finding a place to eat dinner and getting back to our B&B for the night. We piled into our car and 10 miles later, we were at the golf shop at Tain.

Tain is a wonderfully situated links course on the shores of the Cromarty Firth, north of Inverness. Nestled between the sea and the medieval town from which it gets its name, the Tain course was initially laid out in 1890 by none other than Old Tom Morris, and remains one of the great links courses of Scotland. We arrived at 4:00 in the afternoon remembering that, in August, dark doesn't come to Northern Scotland until well after 9:00. It was a glorious afternoon, balmy by Scottish standards. A light breeze off the ocean floated white, puffy clouds across a deep blue sky. The shirt-sleeve temperature might lower enough to require a light sweater as the evening wore on. But could we just drive up and play? On a day like this?

The pro shop attendant was happy to see us. Could we get out right away? No problem, gents. There was a competition scheduled in 30 minutes, but we could start now. If the two fellows playing the match-play competition caught up with our four-ball, would we just stand aside and let them play through? Of course we agreed, and off we went. It was beautiful weather on a Thursday afternoon in August on one of the finest links courses in Scotland, and we were virtually alone on the course! We could see a few other groups out across the course, but the holes in front of us stretched empty of players, and the 2-ball competition that followed us was 30 minutes behind.

Such is the common experience in the Highlands and Islands. A few of the area's most famous courses, notably Royal Dornoch, Nairn, and Nairn Dunbar, do require advanced booking. These courses are experiencing increased play, as they are "discovered" by foreign visitors and are added to the itinerary of some golf tour companies. But other equally top-of-the-line courses such as Machrihanish, Tain, Brora, Golspie, and Machrie are still so remote and undiscovered that they present no problems with finding a tee time. On almost all of the Highlands and Islands courses, the Independent Golfer can just walk on and play, even at the height of the season. And you might find yourself almost alone.

Having said that you can generally walk on to most of these courses, a word of caution is in order. There are some times when walking on any course may be difficult. Most clubs set aside a few hours on one or two days a week as "ladies days." You would want to avoid these, even if you are a woman, because most times will have been booked in advance by the local ladies. Also, because the Scots are generally so keen on competition, all clubs will have some times set aside for sanctioned competitions. For example, during the summer every club generally schedules an "open" on some weekend that any golfer can enter. There are also regularly scheduled inter-club competitions that pit teams from neighboring courses against each other. Finally, local intra-club matches are played throughout the season. If any of this is happening, you will not be able to walk on and play.

Given all of this, it is probably wise to verify that tee times are available at the courses you plan to play. A number of travel books that advise Americans on how to plan golf outings in Scotland recommend that you write ahead to the club secretary requesting a tee time, explaining who you are and assuring them that you are an experienced golfer knowledgeable in the etiquette of play. Such a formal request may have been a requirement in the past but, for most courses, it is no longer necessary. Most of the larger courses have web sites on which you can book tee times with ease. The best way to secure a tee time for any course that doesn't have a website is simply to call by telephone. (To call Scotland from America, dial 011 44 and the course's phone number, dropping the first 0 of that number. You only use that 0 when calling from inside Scotland.) When you place your call, remember that the day in Scotland is five to eight hours later than it is in America, depending upon your time zone here. You will want to call from America in the early morning to reach them in their afternoon. On a few of the smallest courses, the telephone is not monitored. These courses are, of course, the easiest to walk on.

Finally, there is the issue of the single golfer. Can you call as a single and request a tee time? The answer is, absolutely "yes." All but the most high-priced and "snooty" courses will welcome an inquiry from a single golfer. If there is a time in the schedule, you will get it. You might also like to make it clear that you would welcome the opportunity to play with others. Most Scot starters are not in the habit of placing people who don't know each other together, probably because they do not feel the press to fill the course like their American counterparts. They would rather have two or three people who are acquainted enjoy their round together than be saddled with an unknown whose play is questionable. Nevertheless, if you ask, they will make an effort to look for others to play in your time slot with you. I have always enjoyed such pick-up matches with locals, who are typically eager to share stories about their courses and the characters who have played there.

If starting times are tight, starters are also willing to ask a group of two or three if they would mind including you. In such a case, be prepared to offer your handicap when asked. For everybody's sake, they don't want to mis-match people with different abilities.

Playing the Well-Known Courses

All the above notwithstanding, it is certainly understandable that you might want to play the Old Course at St. Andrews or to include in your itinerary one or more of the more famous courses that host the British Open or the Ryder Cup matches. For these, you will need to plan well ahead, seek starting times early and, yes, be prepared to pay for the privilege of playing these courses. The biggest challenge is playing St. Andrews. There are, in fact, six courses administered by the St. Andrews Links Trust, including the Old Course, the New Course, The Jubilee Course, the Eden Course, the Strathtyrum Course, and the nine-hole Balgove Course. A seventh is under construction.

The Old Course is surely the one you want, but be advised: to play it, you will be required to play a second round at another of the St. Andrews courses. Further, a handicap requirement of 24 for men and 36 for women is strictly enforced. You will need to show your valid USGA-Affiliate handicap card.

There are a number of ways to secure a tee time. The first, which is the surest, is to put in a request well ahead of your travel. The emphasis here is on "well ahead." For the main season (between April and October) you must submit your request at least 12 months in advance. Eighteen months is recommended. Advanced requests can be submitted through the Links Trust's website at: **www.standrews.org.uk**.

If you can't do this, you must enter the daily visitor's ballot (lottery). The Trust's management issues about 50% of the available starting times in this manner. You must apply by telephone or in person by 2:00 p.m. for a time on the following day, and you must have a minimum of two golfers applying. They don't take single's applications for the ballot. The results of the lottery are posted on the Trust's website and in various shop windows around town at 4:00 p.m. The management is quick to point out that "Success in the ballot is not guaranteed and chances vary according to the time of year, how busy the course is and the weather."

A third way to play the Old Course is to walk on. It is common for tee times to be given to two or three golfers, leaving slots to be filled by singles. You can show up at the Old Course's Starter's House in the early morning and ask to be put on the list. Play starts at 7:00. Golfers are known to be there as early as 5:30 looking for a time. Because of the long summer days in this northern land, you can also check in just after noon to find a single slot in the late afternoon.

Each day, tee times from 8:00 to 9:00 and from 5:00 to 6:00 are reserved for local golfers. This offers you yet another way to get on. You just need to know a resident of St. Andrews who is willing to take you out. How? If you don't know anybody who lives there (and chances are, you don't) you need to start talking to folks when you arrive – the bartender or patron in the pub in which you eat lunch, the shopkeeper where you purchase a souvenir, or the proprietor of the hotel or guest-house where you are staying. They might know friends who would welcome a visitor. And don't forget that St. Andrews is a university town, and university students play often and for ridiculously low green fees. Find a student and chat him or her up.

There are other, more costly ways of getting on to the Old Course. Hotel packages at the big hotels often include tee times. Some of the more expensive tour packages offer secured tee times. And then there is "The Old Course Experience" (www.oldcourse-experience.com) which puts together tee times, lodging, and meals into a very pricey package that might result in your tee time alone costing you over $1,500.00!

The other well-know courses are only slightly less difficult and expensive to play. Here are examples:

Royal Troon – You are required to pay for and play both their championship course and their second Portland course. Visitors may only play from 9:30 to 11:00 and 2:30 to 4:00 on Mondays, Tuesdays, and Thursdays. Times can be sought on the web: **www.royaltroon.co.uk.**

Muirfield – Visitors can only book times on Tuesdays and Thursdays between 8:40 and 9:50 and, if there are four of you playing, you must start on the 10th tee. The handicap limit for men is 18 and women, 20. Their website is **www.muirfield.org.uk.**

Prestwick – A more forgiving visitors policy here allows you to play weekday mornings and afternoons with the exception of Thursday, which is morning only. No visitors on Saturdays or Bank Holidays, and Sundays offer limited times during summer. You can book your time at: **www.prestwickgc.co.uk.**

Carnoustie – They are eager to attract play, but do not post a general policy for available tee times. Rather, you must submit a request via their website (**www.carnoustiegolflinks.co.uk**) and wait to be told if that time is available. In addition to their Championship course, they offer the Burnside Course and the Buddon Links. There is a handicap restriction of 28 or lower for men and 36 or lower for ladies on the Championship and Burnside courses.

Turnberry – If you do not stay at their Resort Hotel you cannot reserve tee times until two weeks before you want to play. By then, the chance that times will be available is small. You can try at their website: **www.turnberry.co.uk.**

Entering an Open – A Great Way to Enjoy Golf in Scotland

Now I want to share with you one of the most curious, best kept secrets in Scotland about obtaining tee times. It is curious because no Scot intends that this be kept from Americans, yet it must be well-kept because very few Americans know about it. It is simply this. Virtually every course in the Highlands and

Islands holds an Open Competition some time each summer. Depending on the club, the competition may be one to seven days in length. Anybody, including any American, with an established handicap may enter. If you enter, you are guaranteed tee times and will have the opportunity to play with other entrants who are typically Scots and golf-mad like yourself. Add to this, when entering a club's open, you get the thrill of competition play. And finely, best of all, the fee you pay will be LESS than the normal green fee you would pay when playing the course at any other time. Now, is that a deal, or what!

Let me illustrate this with the most prominent club open in the Highlands and Islands, the Carnegie Shield competition at Royal Dornoch. (The Shield itself, one of the oldest trophies in golf, was donated to the club by local-boy-made-good Andrew Carnegie. It is a large silver shield that boasts beautiful engravings of the Dornoch Cathedral, Skibo Castle, and the Bishop's Palace, now the Castle Hotel in Dornoch.) First, you must remember that Royal Dornoch is an absolutely world-class course, one of the very best you would ever play, anywhere.

The competition, which lasts over a full week, has two "flights," one for 120 higher-handicap players (handicap 10 - 21) and one for 150 lower-handicappers (9 and below). Each flight begins with two days of stroke play. The low 32 players qualify for match play that covers three more days. If you don't qualify after the first two days or if you lose in the first round of match play, you can play a one-day consolation competition on Royal Dornoch's 2nd course, the Struie. Further, on the days when the other flight is playing its stroke play qualifying rounds, you can travel 15 miles north for an additional competition at the Golspie Links course.

And now, as if engaging in such a quality competition weren't enough, the deal gets even better. The normal summer green fee for a visitor for a single round at Royal Dornoch is £72 ($122.40) on a weekday or £82 ($139.40) on a weekend. But if you enter the Carnegie Shield competition, all that changes. The total entry fee, green fees and everything, comes to only

£55 ($93.50). That's all. A minimum of three rounds on one of the best courses in the world, with another consolation round if you don't do well on the Struie course, for £55. Friends, it doesn't get any better than this!

Of course, there is the problem of getting in. Needless to say, the Carnegie Shield is very popular in Scotland, and indeed across Great Britain. You must get your entry in very early, probably mid-February, and you may be subject to a drawing for places if the number of entries exceeds the allocated slots. You can obtain all the details from the club's website: **www.royaldornoch.com.**

Though it is probably the most prestigious, the Carnegie Shield is just one of many club opens held by golf clubs across the Highlands and Islands. Others are smaller and of shorter duration, but you can play any of the better courses under competition conditions and at equal monetary savings. For example, the Nairn Dunbar course offers fabulous links golf just east of Inverness along the Moray Firth. It stages a five-day open in August for 200 golfers who play 36 holes of qualifying stroke play. The best 32 players in each of three flights (scratch, low, and high handicap) go on to match play. For the less fortunate, there is a two-day consolation competition. The cost for the whole competition? Just £65 ($110.50).

These competitions offer a wonderful opportunity for the Independent American Golfer. Not being tied to a package tour's schedule, you can plan to stay a few days in one locale in order to participate in a local, competition while taking advantage of substantial savings on green fees. To find a competition that fits your planned travel times, you can go to any club's website. Most feature competition news. A phone call to the course may be necessary to get details and an entry form. Because these club opens are so popular, you should firm up your plans at least six months before the open dates.

To help you in your search for likely club opens, you might also obtain the *Wee Yellow Book*. Published each year, this small paperback lists all the amateur golf events in Scotland, their dates and types of competition, and the phone numbers of the hosting clubs. Generally sold only at golf shops in Scotland, you can obtain one at: **www.weeyellowbook.com**.

The Club and Clubhouse

Most courses in the Highlands and Islands are owned by local golf clubs that also maintain their clubhouses near the first tee. The biggest exceptions to this are the courses that were built years and even centuries ago on "common land" owned by the village or town. In these cases, golf clubs may have been given the right to maintain their clubhouses nearby, as they also assumed the responsibility for running and maintaining the course. In any case, for Scots, their golf club and its clubhouse are indispensable parts of their golfing experience.

Almost all Scots who play golf belong to a golf club. These clubs are neither as elementary as the typical "men's" and "women's" clubs found at all American public courses, nor are they as complex and expensive as American private country clubs. First of all, they are private and membership is somewhat regulated, though the degree of regulation varies tremendously. There are a small number of very exclusive private clubs that impose strict limits based on social status and even gender. Most clubs, especially those in the Highlands and Islands, simply admit anybody who applies. The true requirement is that members share a common love for the game.

Membership in all but the most exclusive clubs is quite cheap by American standards. Most clubs have yearly membership fees ranging between £200 ($340) and £400 ($680) per year and, unlike most American private country clubs, there are no monthly fees. This is so reasonable that it is not uncommon for Scot golfers to maintain membership in two or even three clubs. One membership may be at a course near where they live and the other may be at a larger, more challenging course to which they go on holiday every few weeks.

Club membership brings considerable benefits. First, membership gives you unlimited free play on the course. No additional fees are required. Yes, there are no monthly charges. Little wonder that Scots would rather pay £250 per year than £25 per day to play at their local course. As a member, you can also enter all the club competitions, of which there are many through the season. This fits very well with the Scottish love of competition described above.

Also, a member has the privilege of bringing a guest onto the course. The Scots even have a verb for this, "to guest." If a member "guests" you, he will probably be required to pay a nominal fee that is generally much less than you would be required to pay for the round as a non-member. On many of the smaller courses, things are so loose that the guesting fee is waived or just forgotten. In the larger clubs, obviously because of their popularity, collecting the guesting fee is mandatory, and often members are limited in the number of guests they can bring on in a year. In any event, if you are fortunate enough to play as a guest of a member, you will of course want to offer to reimburse that member for any fees that might have been paid for you.

Finally, as a member, the Scottish golfer has access to the facilities of the clubhouse of which all Scot golfers are rightfully proud. As you might expect, clubhouses vary in quality, but, in general, most feature a club room with comfortable seats and tables which typically look out over the course, a bar and small kitchen that provides an adequate post-round repast, a locker/ changing room with showers, and perhaps a small golf shop in which you can buy things you need for your game and souvenirs or gifts to take home.

The important point for us as visitors to these clubs is that, in virtually every case, when you pay your visitor green fees for the round, you also are purchasing a "membership for the day" in the local club. You are given rights of access to the clubhouse and its facilities to enjoy as the local members do. In all of the clubhouses of the Highlands and Islands, this availability of membership privileges for guests is a genuine and hospitable offer. Members enjoy seeing you enjoy the facilities of which they are rightly proud. They are quick to accept you into conversations in the bar and lounge and to make you feel welcome and at home. The legendary Scottish hospitality for which these friendly people are so well known is nowhere more evident than in the golf clubs of the north.

In the club rooms you will generally find members relaxing, chatting over the day's play. These are comfortable and colorful places that almost always feature lists of past Captains and Club Champions on the walls, perhaps stretching back to the 19th century. The club "treasury," a set of glass cabinets, often displays silver trophies, plaques, and medallions that chronicle long-ago triumphs. Photographs and paintings can be found on the walls depicting the club's and its members' past glories. The furniture is comfortably casual and invites relaxed and informal conversation.

The bar is normally fully licensed, which means that it offers a full range of alcoholic and non-alcoholic beverages. Beer is quite popular, wine less so. There is always a good selection

Courtesy Golf Highlands

The members of the Nairn Golf Club enjoy one of the "poshest" clubhouses in the Highlands and Islands

Courtesy Golf Highlands

The Wick Golf Club is proud of its modest but functional clubhouse that is more typically found across the Highlands and Islands.

of malt whiskies and other liquors on the back bar that the bartender would be happy to pour.

Depending on the size of the club, food may or may not be available to golfers who walk in with no advanced warning. Many of the smaller clubs ask golfers to alert them ahead of time if they would like lunch served after a round. In many larger clubs, such advanced booking is not necessary. It is a good idea to inquire about this when you are making arrangements for your play.

The selection of food is typically limited when compared to a full-service pub or restaurant, but there are always enough choices so that the hungry golfer is not disappointed. A lunch selection might include a homemade soup (almost always hearty and delicious), various sandwiches with the ubiquitous chips (fried potatoes) if you so desire, and perhaps a tuna or chicken salad. Many club restaurants also offer tea in the later afternoon that, of course, comes with some sort of biscuit or shortbread.

Copeland 2006

The clubhouse of the Helmsdale Golf Club. Typical of the smallest courses in the sparsely populated North that continue fiercely to preserve the game for locals and any who chance to visit.

In all but the smallest clubs, members prepare for play in the locker room. They have lockers in which clothing, rain suits, shoes, and clubs are kept. Visitors carry what they need into the locker rooms to prepare. It is generally considered inappropriate to change clothing or shoes in the parking lot. I have found that a small shoe bag is an indispensable piece of equipment for play in Scotland. A good bag not only holds shoes but also a change of socks and underwear for after the round. Most of the middle-to large-sized clubs have showers that are welcome additions to the golfing experience, especially after a cold and blustery day on the course. Towels are typically available as part of your membership privileges.

Changing at least your shoes in the locker room before and after your round solves another problem as well. Though very hospitable in general, clubs do not like members or guests wearing golf shoes, metal- or soft-spiked, into their club rooms. The custom after you finish your round is to go into the locker room, shower if you want, change to your street clothes if you have them but always change your shoes, and then go into the club room for your post-round debriefing. A few of the more exclusive clubs require that you wear a jacket into the club room but this is rare. By contrast, in all club rooms courtesy requires that you take your hat off before you enter.

The "poshness" of these clubhouses does vary across the courses in the Highlands and Islands. A few of the very smallest courses make due with a small, one-room wooden hut – no locker room, no showers, nothing. At the other end, some courses' facilities are very elaborate and convey the feeling of an exclusive resort or spa. Most of the northern courses have quite adequate clubhouses that fall between these extremes. This variation is roughly mirrored by the green fees that clubs charge non-members; the cheaper the fee, the sparser the accommodations. Generally speaking, most Americans are pleasantly surprised by the comfort, friendliness and convenience that Scottish clubhouses offer them as visitors, especially when they consider how little they are paying for the privilege of use.

Getting a Time for Play

The central message here is the great advantage the Independent golfer has when planing a trip to the Highlands and Islands. The beautiful courses of the North are not overrun with tourists. It is easy to schedule a time to play. You can take advantage of the Scots' genuine interest in having you come to enjoy their courses. You can take part in local competitions and you can enjoy the clubhouses and other facilities. It is hard to imagine how a golf trip to Scotland could be better than one planned to include some of the courses of the Highlands and Islands.

To make your planning even more easy, visit the website associated with this book: **www.TheIndependentGolfer.com.**

CHAPTER 5

Playing Golf and Saving Money: Two Great Scottish Traditions

Picture yourself and a few golfing buddies playing the most northern golf course on the mainland of the United Kingdom. Near Cape Wrath, in the far northwest of Scotland, the Durness Golf Club is set in a wild and wonderful place on rolling links-style land with unobstructed views of glacier-sculpted mountains, untouched sandy beaches that stretch off into the distance, and the rolling Atlantic Ocean. You are alone with your golf on Durness; no cities, no towns, no smokestacks, no power lines, nothing to separate you from the magnificence that is the Scottish Highlands. Durness offers one of the most talked-about finishing holes in Scotland, a 3-par that asks you to hit from a tee box on the edge of a cliff and carry the ball 155 yards across the wave-tossed Atlantic Ocean to a green on the opposite cliff that has sand traps on its right and the ocean that stretches to Newfoundland on its left. Durness is a 9-holer, but has the unusual quality of having eighteen tee boxes so that, the second time around, you come at the same greens but from different angles and/or distances. Playing Durness is a considerable challenge and a wonderful experience that you will fondly remember the rest of your life.

Or picture yourself taking a moment on the tee box of #10 at Strathpeffer Spa Golf Club north of Inverness. You look east to the Cromarty Firth and the Black Isle on Scotland's east coast and on to the North Sea beyond. You then turn your gaze 180 degrees to look west toward the Three Sisters of Kintail that rise out of the Atlantic Ocean on the country's west coast. You realize that, with a turn of the head on this magnificent

Courtesy Golf Highlands

At Durness Golf Club, a 9-holer, you play this hole #9 twice. First time around, you hit 108 yards over the Atlantic Ocean to the far green. From different tees for your second round you need to carry it 155 yards.

course, you can see across the entire width of Scotland in one breathtaking panorama. You find it difficult to turn back to the job at hand, hitting your ball 162 yards across a mountain pond to the saucer-shaped green on this beautiful 3-par hole. Hey, it's a tough job, but somebody has to do it. And it might as well be you.

The interesting thing is that you could have neither of these experiences, nor any of hundreds like them, if your golfing holiday in Scotland were taken as a planned tour. None of the golf tours go to Durness or Strathpeffer Spa, or, for that matter, to any of the other 86 wonderfully different courses in the Highlands and Islands of Scotland. The only way to enjoy these courses is to travel there yourself.

As an Independent Golfer, you will find it quite easy to take charge of your own travel in Scotland. Once you decide that you are not going to be limited to the tour routes, a wide range of possibilities opens up to you. You can travel to any number of interesting, challenging, and uncrowded courses that will test your game without testing your patience or your wallet. Getting to these courses might take you over scenic roads that hug rocky coasts, or twist through wooded glens or over heather-covered mountain passes. Following your own timetable, you might decide to interrupt your journey for a few minutes to scramble up the side of a hill to explore an 800-year-old castle ruin that you spied as you came around a curve in the road. Or you might stop off at a local competition of Highland Games to watch dancing troops, pipe bands, sheep dog trials, and local athletes as they toss the caber (throw a 150 lbs, 18 foot long wooden log). You can stop at a pub in a village of 12 houses nestled in a forest along the bank of a mountain loch (lake), there to enjoy a lunch of hearty homemade soup and a ham and cheese sandwich washed down with the local lager. You can select a small hotel or bed-and-breakfast and enjoy an evening cup of tea with the proprietor before snuggling down into crisp sheets under a fluffy down comforter for the night. And you can do

Courtesy Golf Highlands

The views from the higher holes at Strathpeffer Spa are breathtaking.

this all at a fraction of the cost-per-day of any golf tour that you could take.

The economics of tour vs. independent travel are simple. The tour companies must supply you with hotel rooms, green fees, and transportation. They must pay their personnel to "meet and greet" you and guide you around. And then the companies must add their profit to what they charge you.

As an Independent Golfer, you will pay the same green fees as you would on a tour. You could stay at the same hotels that the tours use or you could use less expensive lodgings that are just as clean and welcoming and more personable than the large hotels the tours use. Your transportation might, on average, cost the same as on a tour, but you, not the bus driver, are in control of your schedule. And you don't have to pay the tour company's personnel costs or the profit for which they are in business. The result can be a golf trip that is more exciting and memorable than a packaged tour, and that costs a fraction of what a tour would cost.

Let me illustrate this with two examples. First, going strictly by descriptions and rates that are published on the World Wide Web, I located a mid-level tour called "The Scottish Highlands Tour." For $4,878 per person, double occupancy, you could get nine days and eight nights of travel and play seven rounds of golf at the following courses: Royal Dornoch, Nairn, Cruden Bay, Royal Aberdeen, Montrose, and the Old Course and the Jubilee Course at St. Andrews. You would stay at three different hotels: The Kingsmill Hotel in Inverness, Marcliff at Pitofels in Aberdeen, and the Old Course Hotel in St. Andrews. Transportation would be by a "mid-sized rental car with unlimited mileage" that you would drive yourself. (No busses on this tour; a point for the tour operator.) A full Scottish Breakfast would also be included. You would have to buy all your lunches and dinners, and would pay for gas, additional travel insurance if you wanted it, any car rental taxes that apply, and, of course, any incidentals. (Are you really going to stay out of the pubs and away from the historical sites, cultural exhibitions, and shops and stores?)

Now, with just a little homework on the web, I can determine that the total costs for green fees at these courses per person would total $802.90. Likewise, the total cost for eight nights lodging at the three hotels listed by the tour would be $1,207.40 per person. Finally, the cost of renting a mid-sized car for eight days, say a Citroen C5, would be $458, or $229 per person. This totals $2,239.30. You would have paid the operator $4,878 for this tour, leaving $2638.70. That's a 54% mark-up for the tour operator!

Further, the most attractive part of this tour, a chance to play the Old Course at St. Andrews, is not guaranteed. Rather, in small print on the web page, the tour operator promises only to submit your names for the daily ballot, by which starting times are given to golfers who sign up the day before and keep their fingers crossed that they will be lucky and snag a time. If you aren't lucky, and many people aren't, you will play the Jubilee course instead, and the tour operator promises to submit your name again for the next day's ballot. If you aren't lucky that second day, you won't be playing the Old Course this trip! The point is, if it is worth it to you to pay $2,638.70 extra so that somebody will make your reservations for you, meet you at the airport, shake your hand and point you to the car rental desk, then this tour is for you. But, for many of us, that's a rather steep price for a little convenience.

An even more important point is that an Independent Golfer could plan a similar trip, play more golf, and pay even less. Here is how. First, some changes could be made in the courses played. I would recommend keeping Royal Dornoch and Nairn but would substitute Brora, Tain, Golspie, Boat of Garten and Gullane #1 (this last near Edinburgh to be played the day before your departure) for the others in this tour operator's list. (Yes, I'm not including the Old Course at St. Andrews. If you want to play it, substitute it for Gullane #1 and submit your tee time request 18 months before you plan to go.) I would also schedule two rounds a day on four of these courses. Hey, if you are there, why not play? They are absolutely wonderful courses, equal in every way to the tour operator's originals, but, being in the less-populated north, they are less played, so they can be scheduled easily and they are less expensive. The total cost for playing 11 rounds on these courses would be $547, thus saving $113 while playing four more rounds of golf.

I would also recommend that the Independent Golfer forego the rather pricey hotels offered by the tour operator and instead use the wonderfully welcoming Bed and Breakfast lodgings available in the Highlands. The eight nights could average $40 per night, totaling $320 in contrast with the $1,332 that you would have paid for the tour's hotels. Adding in the same rental car costs, this trip would cost the Independent Golfer $1,096. The result would be a savings of $3,782 and four more rounds of golf compared to the tour's price. Why would anybody want to do anything else?

To make the case crystal clear, here is another example, this time a lower-end but, in some ways, more imaginative tour. This operator offers the "Highlands and Islands Golf Tour" for $2,400. It offers nine rounds of golf in seven days at Machrihanish (2 rounds), Machrie (3 rounds), Royal Dornoch, Nairn, Moray (Old Course), and Forres. I must say I like the idea of playing two rounds at Machrihanish and three at Machrie. These are great golf courses. They deserve all the time you can give them.

This tour will have you sleep in five hotels for nine nights: The Cairnbaan Hotel in Lochgilphead, the Machrie Hotel on the island of Islay, Morangie House in Tain, and the Knockomie Hotel in Forres. (For some reason, this tour operator has you stay two nights in Tain without playing the Tain Golf Club's wonderful course, which would offer a much better experience than either Moray or Forres.) The same circumstances concerning rental car transportation apply. The operator also states that you will have "Day membership of golf clubs including use of the club house." This is hardly an added benefit. Any golfer who pays green fees at any club in Scotland is, in fact, purchasing a daily club membership with all the benefits of clubhouse use attached. The tour has added nothing here.

Looking on the web to find green fees, hotel costs, and transportation, I find that, if they were purchased separately, they would total $1,721. You would have paid the tour operator a profit of $678 to do that airport greeting.

Further, an Independent Golfer could make a few changes in the courses played (I would substitute Brora and Tain for Old Moray and Forres and play two rounds on each of them), use Bed and Breakfast lodgings, and do the whole trip for $1,355, a savings of $1,045 over the tour price.

All it takes is a little planning and a bit of an adventurous willingness to step out on your own. There are, of course, traveling golfers who are not willing to take such initiative. They need to have all the planning done for them, perhaps because they actually don't know how easy it is to plan a wonderful golfing trip. Tour companies actually do little that a capable golfer can't do himself or herself, if willing. All you need is some good information, a sense of what to expect, and some basic ideas about how to proceed.

In the following pages, I offer advice that should allow you to enjoy golf in the Highlands and Islands independently, save considerable money, and, as I did, come back and tell your friends about what a fabulous and unforgettable experience such a trip can be.

Playing From a Hub

You need to have a basic strategy to guide your trip-planning, and I suggest that you plan to "play from a hub." On our first experience in Scotland some thirty years ago, my wife and I rented a car and traveled the back roads of the Highlands, stopping each night to stay in a Bed and Breakfast establishment in a different village. We saw some fantastic scenery and

I played some fabulous courses, but we made one serious mistake. Staying every night in a different location, we spent a considerable amount of time each day packing and unpacking our bags, carrying them to and from the car, and stuffing them into space that wasn't designed to carry as much as we had. Two people's luggage and my golf clubs (yes, my wife doesn't play) make for a number of trips between room and car, and a lot of stuffing. We also needed to take some time each afternoon to look for that evening's lodging. We found that it is best to locate a place to stay for the night by the mid-afternoon, especially in the smaller, more out-of-the way places that we wanted to visit. All the above severely cut into our travel and sightseeing time, not to mention my time on the course. The mid-afternoon is much better spent playing golf than searching for a Bed and Breakfast to stay at that evening.

Finally, growing tired of the routine, we decided to stay put in one place for three days. What a relief. After a breakfast at our leisure, we had the whole day to do what we wanted. Scotland is a small country, and we found that we could drive a good distance, see sights or play golf, and then return to our "hub" with ease. No wrestling with bags, no hunting new lodging each day. We also got to know our hosts and spent a pleasant evening playing cribbage and sharing stories of travel.

I highly recommend that, on a golfing outing in Scotland, the Independent Golfer pick a "hub" for operations from which travel to the desired courses is easy. If the trip is short, five to seven days, one hub is sufficient. You can get around to all the golf you want from one place in that time. If you are lucky enough to be staying longer, then two hubs might work, staying in one area for the first half of your trip and another for the second. For two-week trips, I have tried both a two-hub and a three-hub plan. Though three hubs might appear to be more ambitious and offer more opportunities, I actually found the two-hub plan was more relaxed, gave me more time away from the road, and offered just as much opportunity for great golf.

If you opt for this "hub strategy," selecting an advantageous hub is all-important. Two friends of mine on a week of golf in Scotland were able to take advantage of an acquaintance's apartment outside of Glasgow as their base. Their plan was to stay there at no expense and to drive a rental car each day to a different course that they wanted to play. They knew Scotland to be a small country (at 30,414 square miles, it is smaller than South Carolina) and thought the driving would be tolerable. They were wrong. Their abiding memories of that trip are not

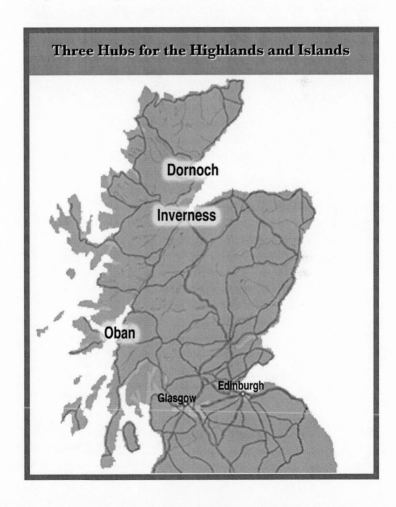

Three Hubs for the Highlands and Islands

the courses they played but the highways they drove, the traffic cones they encountered that marked road construction work, and the traffic jams they worked through trying to get to the courses they wanted to play.

Their difficulty was that Glasgow is a poorly-situated hub from which to play golf. The courses that they wanted to play were all a considerable distance from their apartment. Most required them to drive through the city in morning rush-hour traffic on motorways clogged with commuting Glaswegians, whom they met again in the evening as they returned. After

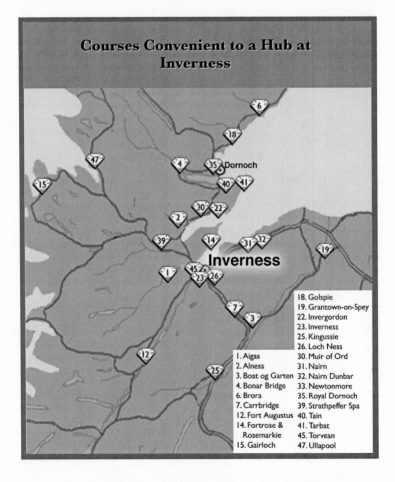

Courses Convenient to a Hub at Inverness

Dornoch

Inverness

1. Aigas	18. Golspie
2. Alness	19. Grantown-on-Spey
3. Boat og Garten	22. Invergordon
4. Bonar Bridge	23. Inverness
6. Brora	25. Kingussie
7. Carrbridge	26. Loch Ness
12. Fort Augustus	30. Muir of Ord
14. Fortrose & Rosemarkie	31. Nairn
15. Gairloch	32. Nairn Dunbar
	33. Newtonmore
	35. Royal Dornoch
	39. Strathpeffer Spa
	40. Tain
	41. Tarbat
	45. Torvean
	47. Ullapool

their trip was over, they admitted that the free rent they enjoyed while using their friend's apartment was not worth the time and aggravation that came from the driving they had to do.

They would have had a much more enjoyable time if they had found a hub that was centered among a cluster of courses that they wanted to play. If you are playing in the Highlands and Islands, there are three natural clusters of courses that offer superb opportunities for establishing your hub: Inverness, Dornoch and Oban.

Inverness

In the north-east, you will find the city of Inverness ideally centered for easy access to great golf. Royal Dornoch, a course that all critics agree is one of the very best courses in the world, is just 45 minutes up the A9, an easily-traveled, two-lane road with no city traffic. Just south of Royal Dornoch is Tain, one of the best links courses in the Highlands. Also to the north, but even closer to Inverness, are Fortrose and Rosemarky, Strathpeffer Spa, Invergorden, Muir of Ord, and Alness, each offering a delightfully different but challenging opportunity for a rich Highland golf experience. Nairn, one of the most upscale courses in the Highlands, is just a few miles east of Inverness, as is its neighbor Nairn Dunbar. To the south and west, you will find a number of lesser known but wonderful courses that are "must plays," including Boat of Garten, Kingussie, Newtonmore, Grantown-on-Spey, and the little 9-holer at Aigas. Finally, in Inverness itself, you will find three courses: Inverness, Torvean, and Loch Ness.

The city of Inverness offers a wide variety of hotels, B&Bs, and self-catering apartments that are well maintained and reasonably priced. Though it is considered "The Capital" of the Highlands, Inverness is a small city with only about 65,000 inhabitants. It was recently ranked 5th among 189 British cities and towns for its quality of life. The city is centered around its medieval castle, where legend has it that MacBeth, of Shakespeare notoriety, built his stronghold. The city has a

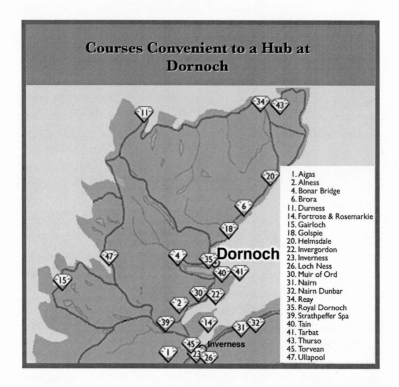

Courses Convenient to a Hub at Dornoch

1. Aigas
2. Alness
4. Bonar Bridge
6. Brora
11. Durness
14. Fortrose & Rosemarkie
15. Gairloch
18. Golspie
20. Helmsdale
22. Invergordon
23. Inverness
26. Loch Ness
30. Muir of Ord
31. Nairn
32. Nairn Dunbar
34. Reay
35. Royal Dornoch
39. Strathpeffer Spa
40. Tain
41. Tarbat
43. Thurso
45. Torvean
47. Ullapool

delightful winding of old streets through its shopping center which has been blocked off from motor traffic to allow leisurely pedestrian access. Of course, it sports a typically Scottish selection of pubs, clubs, and other evening entertainments. It is situated at the mouth of the Caledonian Canal that connects Loch Ness and the Great Glen with the Moray Firth and the North Sea, and thus offers scenic, canal-side walks with views of a diverse range of wildlife, gardens, and beautiful vistas of mountains and sea.

Dornoch

Because of all the wonderful courses located to the north of Inverness, it might make sense to make the Royal Burgh of Dornoch your base. Royal Dornoch's Championship course will likely top your list and might be played twice. You could get to many of the courses found between Inverness and Dornoch just as easily as you could from an Inverness base, and you could more easily access Golspie and Brora that are just a few minutes to the north. Finally, if you are really adventurous, you could get to the far northern coast and play Durness and Reay, though it might be best to approach these courses as an overnight trek.

Royal Burgh of Dornoch would be a quiet, out-of-the-way home of under 2,500 folks if it wasn't also home to one of the very best golf courses in the world. The village itself is a charming group of old sandstone cottages that cluster around the 13th Century cathedral with its associated bishop's palace (now a hotel) and town jail (now an upscale shop.) It sports sufficient hotels (5), Bed and Breakfasts, and self-catering apartments to meet the needs of any Independent Golfer, but not enough to support large-scale tourism. All the better for us!

Besides golf, visitors enjoy walks on Dornoch's sandy beaches, view wildlife in the nearby National Nature Reserve, hear the Saturday evening outdoor concerts of the local Pipe Band, or even get married (Madonna did!).

Oban

In the west Highlands and Islands, your best base will be the town of Oban. The courses are a bit more scattered here. Some are in relatively remote areas of the mountains and rugged coasts that are scalloped by sea lochs and rivers. Others are on islands that require you to reach them on a ferry. To the south of Oban, down the A83 along the peninsula of Kintyre, is Machrihanish, the crown jewel of the western courses. This course is the ideal goal around which a golf trip to the west Highlands and Islands should be planned. In this area, you will also find the Machrie course on the Island of Islay. It is a two-hour ferry trip and an overnight on the island would be advisable, but the course is worth it. You will always remember your time on the Machrie. Here are also Dunaverty, Tarbert, Inveraray, and Lochgilphead, all wonderful little courses that you must play if you are in their area.

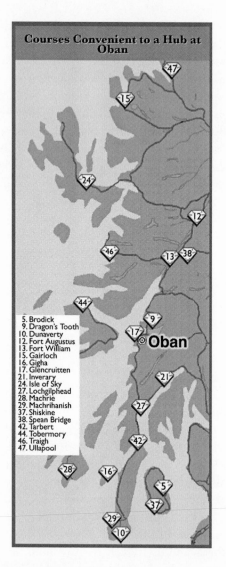

Courses Convenient to a Hub at Oban

5. Brodick
9. Dragon's Tooth
10. Dunaverty
12. Fort Augustus
13. Fort William
15. Gairloch
16. Gigha
17. Glencruitten
21. Inverary
24. Isle of Sky
27. Lochgilphead
28. Machrie
29. Machrihanish
37. Shiskine
38. Spean Bridge
42. Tarbert
44. Tobermory
46. Traigh
47. Ullapool

To the north of Oban are the Dragon's Tooth and Fort William courses within easy driving distance. Farther on are Gairloch, Ullapool, and the courses of the northern coast, Durness, Reay, and Thurso. These last are wonderfully wild and special places but are relatively isolated. A day-trip from Oban to play them would be stretching it. Getting there is best approached as an over-nighter. Finally, the Isle of Skye Golf Club and the Tobermory course on the Isle of Mull offer wonderful island golf.

The harbor town of Oban, which itself sports the Glencruitten golf course, has only 8,500 inhabitants but serves as a tourist center and gateway to the western islands of Scotland. Caledonian MacBrayne ferries leave Oban for the islands of Islay, Colonsay, Coll, Tiree, Mull, Lismore, Barra, and South Uist. The town itself has many hotels and Bed and Breakfast accommodations, and more can be found along the A85, A816, and A828 highways that converge on Oban. Visitors to Oban enjoy the many sightseeing possibilities offered in the area's sea and mountains and its world-famous art glass manufacturing. You must walk just north of town to explore the ruins of Dunollie castle. Without paying any admission fee, you can climb up to and walk around the fortress seat of the MacDougal clan, the Lords of Lorne, who once ruled a third of Scotland from this rocky perch.

What You Get

Traveling as an Independent Golfer, you can certainly save money. But selecting an appropriate hub, staying in a Bed and Breakfast, and traveling each day to play a selection of the courses of the Highlands and Highlands gives you so much more. Most importantly, you gain access to some of the most memorable golfing experiences you will have in your life on courses that are equal to any in their history, tradition, challenge, subtlety and beauty. You will play amid scenic splendor of mountain, forest, coast and sea that is unsurpassed anyplace in the world. You may meet and be befriended by local Scot golfers who are eager to share with you the glories of their national game. And you will do it all under your own control, at your pace and with companions you select. This is the life of the Independent Golfer.

CHAPTER 6

First, Look Right!

The most popular transportation choice for Independent Golfers is the rental car. Because golfers tend to want to spend most of their time on courses rather than waiting for trains or busses, public transportation may not always work out to be the best choice. Rentals give you complete control over your travel. You can change your plans, for example, so that you can stay and play a second round on a course that you just fell in love with without worrying about catching that last train of the day back to the village in which you are staying.

The cost of rental cars is about as reasonable as you would find at home, but be warned, the cars tend to be smaller than we are accustomed to. The advantage is that these smaller cars get very good gas mileage, a welcome feature where gas can cost over $5.00 per gallon. The disadvantage is space. Two golfers with their suitcases and their clubs take up more space in a car than you might think. A group of four will probably need a mini-van or at least a station wagon. It is quite possible to rent a car that is very inexpensive, that gets great gas mileage but that is incapable of carrying all your stuff. Of course, rental agencies will want to rent you as large a car as they can and so their advice might tend toward more than you need. One approach is to book (reserve) a car that may be a bit small and then try to stuff your luggage into it in the rental car parking lot. If it doesn't fit, walk back in and inquire about the possibility of an upgrade.

All the large rental car companies that we know in the U.S. operate in Scotland. If you are comfortable with them, fine, but you should know that there is a much less- expensive alternative. There are a few Scotland-only rental agencies, including DCH Scotland Ltd. and AMK Self Drive, that offer considerable savings over their larger, international competitors. The best known of these is Arnold Clark (see their website: **www.arnoldclark.co.uk**). It is actually the largest auto dealership in Scotland, but they do car rentals too. One reason that agencies like Arnold Clark are less expensive is that they are "off-airport" that is, they don't have to pay the costs of maintaining operations at the major airports of Glasgow and Edinburgh. When they know you are arriving, they will send a car to pick you up at the airline terminal and take you to their car park which is nearby. Their prices are consistently more reasonable than those offered by the major international agencies, and their personnel are always easy to work with.

Driving in Scotland

Every American knows that, if you rent a car in Scotland, you will need to drive on the left side of the road. This is, in fact, not as daunting a requirement as you might be led to believe. After all, once you are on a highway, driving down the left side with oncoming cars whizzing past you on your right, it is not really difficult to remember to stay on the left. You can get the hang of this in the first 10 seconds.

The problems come when you try to get onto the highway in the first place. My wife and I had been in Scotland for about an hour. We had signed all the rental papers, loaded our Nissan Micra with our luggage, adjusted the seats and rear view mirrors, and found the exit from the rental car park onto the frontage road. I carefully looked left to verify that oncoming traffic was clear and then began to inch out onto the road, dutifully aiming at the traffic lane farthest to the left. Just as my wife screamed, I looked right to see the huge flat front of a double-decker bus bearing down on our tiny car. Stomping the break and stalling the engine, I got the car stopped in time to allow the bus driver to swerve around us and go on his way, undoubtedly cursing at the bloody foreigner who almost put him well behind his schedule.

The exits from rental car lots may be the most dangerous places for American drivers in all of the UK. As a driver new to this left-side-of-the-road thing, it is not enough to think through where you should be going. You also need to be aware of where those other cars are coming from. You need to change your driving habits, like that one about looking to the left first for oncoming traffic. You need to look to the right and not the left as you enter an intersection. That's where they'll be coming from.

Another feature of driving in Scotland that is unusual for most Americans is the roundabout. Roundabouts turn out to be an efficient and even clever way of allowing cars from different directions to pass safely through an intersection with the least disruption. With a roundabout at an intersection, you never have to wait at a red light when no cross-traffic is present.

Roundabouts come in all sizes. The typical one is a two-lane road laid out as a large circle, perhaps 40 yards across, with streets entering/exiting it from four different directions. You might come across small or mini-roundabouts that are nothing more than white 8-foot circles painted in the middle of a city intersection. Roundabouts get very large, too, including double circles, each bringing together multiple roads, connected by a feeder road between the circles.

No matter what their size, two simple rules must always be followed. First, as you enter a roundabout, yield the right-of-way

Copeland 2006

Typical Roundabout   Mini-Roundabout

to any traffic that is already in the roundabout. This is relatively easy as long as you remember that those in the roundabout will be coming from your right. Second, if you are in the roundabout, accept without hesitation the right-of-way over cars that are entering. Here is where cautious drivers make mistakes. Nothing exasperates local drivers more than a foreigner in a roundabout who slows down to allow another car to enter.

The other thing that American drivers need to get accustomed to is where most of the car is when they are seated in the driver's seat. Unlike at home, most of the mass of the car in out on your left, not your right. Three Independent Golfer friends and I had just finished a wonderful late afternoon round on Prestwick St. Nicholas and wanted to make some photo memories of our time there. We recalled a beautiful setting that we had seen earlier in the day. It included the 3rd green, a picturesque old stone building that had served as the house of the greenskeeper in former years, and the sea beyond. The Prestwick St. Nicholas course, like many towns' links courses, runs in a narrow band along the coast between the sea and the town. Also, like many links courses, it is bisected by a small road, which gives townsfolk access across the course to the sea. We decided to find that road, get back to the 3rd green, and take our pictures.

Though we had been leaving the driving up to Orin, who had a lot of experience on UK roads, Nick wanted to try his hand at driving and volunteered to drive this one. It was a short distance. Sure, why not? We worked our way through the neighborhood with Nick behind the wheel and found the road that crossed the course to end by the 3rd green. Nick took a rather broad, sweeping right-hand turn onto that road and, wham, the front-left wheel of our car smashed into the stone curb on the road's left. An elderly gentleman, who happened to be walking with his dog along the path just beyond the curb, jumped, his dog cowering behind him. A moment of silence in our car was followed by nervous laughter as we drove on. What happened? Guess I didn't know the left-front wheel was so far over there. Man, did you see that old guy jump?

We found the 3rd green and its adjacent stone building and had our Kodak moment. It was a beautiful sunset, the end to a wonderful day. As we walked back to the car we came upon that same old gentleman, standing with his dog by our car. He was holding our hubcap prominently in his hand. We hadn't noticed that it had been dislodged when Nick found the curb with our wheel. With a wry and knowing smile that said more about his opinion of foreigners' driving than any words could, he handed the hubcap to Nick and turned toward the beach to resume his walk. A left hand raised in a slight wave as he showed his back to us and walked away was his silent goodbye.

I have been told that car rental agents in the UK, when checking a car in from a rental to a foreigner, go first to the left front of the car looking for scratches, dents, bent wheel rims and, yes, missing hubcaps. This most common damage results when the driver doesn't appreciate how far out to the left the car extends. I know that my wife, riding in the passenger seat on the left, has a habit of making a small flipping gesture by rolling her right hand at the wrist, this intended to get me to move the car away from the left edge and more toward the center of the lane in which we are traveling. Seeing her hand flip, I would jog to the right but then protest, "I'm OK. I know where the road is." But I also secretly know she is possibly right. I have probably drifted too far toward the left. It takes an effort to remember that, sitting behind the wheel in Scotland, your eyes should be aligned with the right side of your lane, not the left. There is a lot of car out on your left that you are accountable for. This is a lesson Nick and my buddies will never forget. I will always be thankful to that old gentleman who surely saved us some money by bringing us the hubcap that we might not have missed until the rental agent called it to our attention.

The problem with the location of the left-front of the car is apparently wide-spread among American golfers. I have four good friends who have taken independent golf trips to Scotland for the last nine summers. They rent a car, share the driving duties, and count "curbies." Whenever the driver inadvertently hits a curb with his left-hand tires, he gets a curbie. At the end of the day, anybody who has collected a curbie must buy the others a round of drinks wherever they alight for their evening meal. I don't know if playing this game has actually reduced my friends encounters with objects along the left side of the road, but it is their effort to make Scotland a little safer for the locals, and save to themselves from paying penalties to the car rental agencies in the bargain.

Signage

Scotland, like all of Europe, uses the typical international traffic sign system that features diagrams and numbers and avoids words. Fortunately, most Americans are familiar with this system or can figure out the meaning of any signs they don't yet know. However, there are a few unusual things that are not readily apparent and deserve a bit of advance preparation. The best time to try to discover the meanings of these pavement markings and signs is not when you are behind the wheel, in traffic.

1. As you drive down the road, the pavement markings that follow you include:

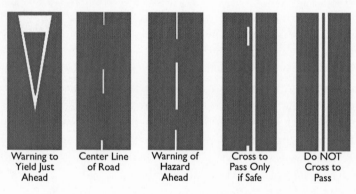

| Warning to Yield Just Ahead | Center Line of Road | Warning of Hazard Ahead | Cross to Pass Only if Safe | Do NOT Cross to Pass |

Of special interest in this group is the triangle at the left. For Scots, it indicates that one is approaching an intersection at which one must be prepared to yield the right-of-way. For Americans, it has an additional meaning. If, while turning into a crossroad at an intersection, you encounter one of these triangles in your lane, blunt end first with the point reaching out in front and away from you, it's time to panic. This ISN'T your lane. Get into the lane to the left, NOW!

2. When you arrive at an intersection, the pavement markings that cross the road in front of your car include:

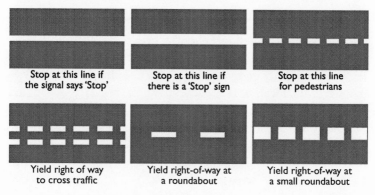

| Stop at this line if the signal says 'Stop' | Stop at this line if there is a 'Stop' sign | Stop at this line for pedestrians |
| Yield right of way to cross traffic | Yield right-of-way at a roundabout | Yield right-of-way at a small roundabout |

3. Some road signs that may be unfamiliar to you include:

| Observe the National Speed Limit | No Waiting | No Stopping | Yield Right of Way | Sharp Turn (to left) | Roundabout Ahead |

Concerning the sign at the left above about the National Speed Limit, it is good to know that, if a speed limit is not posted, the following applies: The speed limit in town is 30 mph. Outside of town on two-lane roads (single carriage-ways) it is 60 mph, and on divided roads (dual carriage-ways) it is 70 mph. Scottish police are serious about speed limits and make extensive use of speed cameras. If you are not careful, a photo might appear in your mail with an accompanying citation when you return from your golfing trip.

The only thing police are more concerned about than speeding is drunk driving. If they suspect you are driving after drinking, they will take you in to the station. No questions: into the pokey you will go. It is simple. Rather than ruin what would otherwise be a wonderfully memorable golfing trip in the Highlands and Islands, make it a point not to get behind the wheel after you drink alcohol.

Ferries

If you drive in the west, you will probably want to take a ferry to some destination. The Machrie course on the Isle of Islay, Tobermory on Mull and Shiskin, Brodick and Corrie on Arran all can only be reached by ferry. Caledonian MacBrayne (known to the locals as CalMac) runs all the regularly-scheduled ferry services in the Highlands and Islands. The timetables and fares are set well ahead and adhered to with punctuality so that planning a passage by ferry can be as dependable as it is adventurous. All the information you need can be found at CalMac's website: **www.calmac.co.uk**. You should pay special attention to the series of packaged deals they offer tourists. One, called the "Island Hopscotch", offers special combinations at reduced cost. Another, the Island Rover, allows flexible travel on any routes for 8 or 15 days. Generally, the CalMac ticket agents are eager to help you find the best deal for your needs. Don't hesitate to ask how you might save money.

It is a good idea to reserve your spot on a ferry ahead of time. This is a working enterprise that services local needs, including large freight trucks. If you show up at the dock and the boat is full, there will not be another for hours or even days. Plan and book ahead.

Alternatives to Rental Cars

To get around Scotland, there are choices other than rental cars. You really have a choice between spending money for a rental car and traveling rapidly or spending less but investing more time in getting there. The cheapest travel in Scotland is by bus and train. You can get anywhere in Scotland by Citylink Bus. (See their website: **www.citylink.co.uk.**) The fares are very reasonable, and they are quite good at keeping to their schedule. However, as with all bus service, you must conform to their timetable, and this might mean waiting for some time between connections.

ScotRail offers the faster and still reasonably-priced alternative of traveling by train between larger destinations. They also offer "Explore Scotland" packages that allow you the freedom to hop-on and hop-off a specified number of times within a set number of consecutive days. (See their website: **www.scotrail.co.uk.**)

CHAPTER 7

Bide a Wee

Mike and Mo met on an oil rig in the middle of the North Sea. They were both young, single, looking for adventure, and wanted to make some good money. They found love. Both worked out of Aberdeen, Mike as a rigger on the platform and Mo as a cook in the platform's galley. They had each other and were setting aside a good nest egg, but they both missed golf. Wanting to get closer to the links, they left their North Sea lives and used their savings to buy a Bed and Breakfast just outside of Oban on the west coast of Scotland. The port of Oban is the end of the rail line and start of ferry service to the Western Isles. It thus attracts loads of tourists and is a perfect place to make a Bed and Breakfast business work. It doesn't hurt that, just a short way from their place, Mike and Mo can play golf at Glencruitten Golf Club, Oban's local course.

Life is good for Mike and Mo. They have a steady stream of guests with whom they enjoy chatting about world travel and golf. While Mo spends the first part of her mornings in the kitchen preparing the Full Scottish Breakfast that they serve their guests, Mike waits in the dining room, eager to hear that your night went well and to offer advice about ferry schedules, local sightseeing attractions, and places to eat dinner. They encourage any of their guests, who are so inclined, to play golf with them at Glencruitten and enjoy showing off their little course when they can. They work hard all season but take their payoff come November when they close their place and move to an apartment in Portugal that they rent every winter. And, yes, you guessed it, their Portuguese place is located about 120 yards

from the 5th tee of a neat little course that they enjoy while the
North Atlantic gales howl back home.

B&B's

Mike and Mo are typical of an increasing number of Bed
and Breakfast proprietors in Scotland. In years past, a B&B was
typically a family house with a spare room, perhaps conveniently
located on a road entering or leaving town. It may have been
that the children in the family had grown up and left their rooms
vacant or the proprietor was a widow looking to make ends
meet. In any event, letting (renting) a room was convenient for
the traveler and the proprietor. Now, more and more, Bed and
Breakfasts are businesses, remodeled houses that let three or four
rooms and are run by ambitious young couples who often have
day jobs as well as their hostelry work.

B&B's are substantially different in Scotland from what we
are accustomed to here in America, where the B&B phenomenon
is both more recent and more expensive. We tend to think of a
Bed and Breakfast as a small, upscale lodge that justifies its high
prices by offering personal attention, high quality surroundings
and welcome alternative to the bustle and noise of commercial
hotels. Antique furnishings, including four-poster beds and
never-actually-used chamber pots, are common. Wine and
cheese are typically served in the evenings, and breakfasts might
include Eggs Benedict or omelets with exotic fillings.

Scottish B&B's are much simpler and, thankfully, much less
expensive. But that is not to say that they are any less desirable
places to stay. We might consider them to be furnished with
wonderful antiques. The difference is that these antiques had
not been recently purchased at considerable cost at an up scale
antique dealer's shop but rather had been in the family, perhaps
since they were new. The quaintness of many Scottish B&B's
is not the result of a talented architect's artful design. Two
hundred year old stone buildings with vine-covered walls that
overlook mountain streams just tend to be quaint.

The important thing is that, whether offering a single room in a family home or three rooms in a small business, Scottish B&B's are typically clean, comfortable, quiet, and accommodating. The hosts are invariably friendly, helpful, and courteous and, thankfully, the rooms they offer are among the most inexpensive accommodations that can be found in Scotland. Costs range between £18 ($30.60) and £25 ($42.50) per person per night, and, as the name says, that includes breakfast! Little wonder that Bed and Breakfast establishments tend to be the preferred accommodation for Independent Golfers.

There is one clear difference that distinguishes B&B rooms from each other. Some have attached restroom facilities with shower or bath that are intended for the exclusive use of those in that room while, in other rooms, you must go down the hall to a shared bathroom. The term that describes self-contained rooms with private facilities is *en suite*, a term that is now as Scottish as it was once Continental. *En suite* rooms tend to be three to five pounds per night more than rooms with only shared facilities.

When selecting a B&B, it is entirely appropriate to ask to see the room and look for a few qualities that may or may not be important to you. An increasing number of B&B's now have televisions in each room while some still retain the older custom of offering a television for guest viewing in the house's parlor. You may see in many bedrooms tea/coffee-making facilities, including a selection of teas and some biscuits or crackers. The beds, of course, will vary. Like other taller Independent Golfers, I always check that the bed does not have a footboard that will inhibit my feet from hanging over the bed's end, making it too short for me to sleep comfortably. Many B&B's now label their rooms "smoking" or "non-smoking," though this is a relatively new custom. Most B&B's will have a pay phone in the parlor but no phones in their rooms. Finally, it is important to ask about payment. Some B&B's will accept credit cards unreservedly while others will add a small surcharge for the card's use. Still others require cash payment.

B&B hosts like to make you feel as if you are staying in your own home. When you rent a room for the night in a B&B, it is common to receive a key to the room and another key to the house's front door which is typically locked around 11:00 each evening. In this way, you have the freedom to go and come as you please without disturbing the hosts. You will have access to the house's parlor where you may sit and read in the evening or chat with the host or with other house guests. The host may brew a pot of tea and invite you to partake, but it is entirely appropriate to decline if you are tired and only care about a long soak in the bath before bed.

Guest Houses

Other types of accommodation can be found throughout Scotland. Guest Houses, slightly larger than B&B's, are commercial businesses that will have a minimum of four letting rooms. The day-to-day business may be conducted by the owner or by hired staff. Some of these rooms will be *en suite* while others not. Breakfast is typically available, and they may also offer evening meals. For comparable value, a Guest House may charge a pound or two more than a B&B per night.

Hotels

Small Hotels have a minimum of six and a maximum of twenty letting rooms and are generally owned independently by proprietors who pride themselves in imposing their personal style on their establishment. At least 50% of the rooms will typically be *en suite*. It is common for Small Hotels to be licensed, that is, to have a bar that serves alcoholic beverages. They will normally serve breakfast, lunch and dinner. It is important to inquire as to whether any meals are included in the cost of the room. In addition to food and drink, Small Hotels may have amenities like telephones in rooms and laundry service.

Next up in scale is a regular Hotel with at least 20 letting rooms, most of which will be *en suite*. Like their small brethren, they will be licensed and offer a full range of meals.

Resort Hotels

At the top of the food chain is the International Resort Hotel that owns or offers access to a wide range of recreational, sporting and leisure facilities, including an 18-hole golf course, swimming, and other "country pursuits" such as fishing, mountain walking, or hunting. As you might guess, these resorts have achieved very high quality ratings for accommodation and service and are quite expensive.

The Accommodation Rating System

Speaking of quality ratings, VisitScotland (formally the Scottish Tourist Board) works very hard to inspect and rate all establishments in their country that offer accommodations to tourists. Their system involves assigning one to five stars, 1 being "fair and acceptable," 2 representing "good," 3 representing "very good," 4 standing for "excellent," and 5 reserved for those that are "exceptional, world class."

In assigning these ratings, they state that their purpose is to give you as clear an indication as possible of the cleanliness, ambience, hospitality, service, accommodation standard and food that you will encounter in the establishment. Places with more stars tend to charge more money.

Self-Catering

The best-kept accommodation secret in Scotland is the self-catering house or apartment. You can find a house, cottage, apartment, or chalet that can be rented by the week, generally from Saturday to Saturday, at a rate that is considerably less than you would pay for each member of your group to stay a week in a B&B. These typically have two to four bedrooms as well as a family room and a complete kitchen. Most have laundry facilities. Almost all come with bed linens and bath towels, but you should inquire about this when making your arrangements. Self-Catering places are ideal for a group of two to eight Independent Golfers who want to base in a particular area for a week and can time their arrival for a Saturday.

Copeland 2006

The Author's wife, Susan, in front of the self-catering cottage we rented by the week in Dornoch. The blue plaque by the door indicates that it is the birthplace of golf course architect Donald Ross.

My wife and I recently spent seven weeks in a self-catering cottage in Dornoch. It was in the center of the village, a half block from the town square and cathedral and an eight-minute walk to the Royal Dornoch Golf Club. It had two bedrooms upstairs and a sitting room, dining room and kitchen down. The cost was £220 ($374) per week, or a little over £15 ($25.50) each night. This is much less than the approximately £46 ($78.20) per night that we would have had to spend for the both of us in a B&B. Further, when our daughters visited us for a week, they could stay in the 2nd bedroom for no additional expense. We were able to save even more money by cooking most of our own meals. Finally, as a golfer, I found most attractive the fact that our cottage was the birthplace of Donald Ross (1872), the great golf course architect who left Dornoch for America in 1899 and subsequently designed 413 courses here, including Pinehurst No. 2 in North Carolina, Seminole in Florida, and Oakland Hills, the site of the 1996 U.S. Open outside Detroit. I don't know if sleeping in a house with Donald's ghost helped my game, but, like most golfers, I'll try anything.

Making Reservations

Booking accommodations ahead of time is a personal thing. Some Independent Golfers enjoy the freedom of waiting until they arrive at a destination before eyeballing available places and making their selection for the night. Others welcome the assurance that they will have a bed secured and waiting for them when they arrive.

In every city and town in the country, VisitScotland has offices that offer regional accommodation listings. For a small fee, they will call ahead and book a place for you. VisitScotland offices also stock two government publications that are quite helpful when seeking accommodations: *Where to Stay: Bed and Breakfast* and *Where to Stay: Hotels and Guest Houses*. Both are revised each year, so be sure to get the most recent edition

Most Independent Golfers learn that it is, in fact, not necessary to book ahead if you are willing to look around for a B&B or Guest House once you arrive. The only exceptions would be if you are traveling on national or bank holidays (during which times accommodations become scarce) or if you wanted a particular Resort Hotel or other popular accommodation.

The exception to the above is booking self-catering apartments or houses. These must be reserved well ahead of time, as they are let for the full week and are popular among vacationers from across the UK. The best way to do this is over the internet. Typically, any area in which you want to base your golf trip will have a visitors' website. Dornoch, Inverness and Oban all have them (**www.visitdornoch.com, www.inverness-scotland.com** and **www.oban.org.uk**.) The Tourist Bureau also maintains a large website that covers the entire country: **www.visitscotland.net**.

Finally, there are other sites that can be of help as well: **www.smoothhound.co.uk** **www.aboutscotland.com** and **www.theaa.com**. Once on the website, it is no trick to locate "accommodations" or "places to stay" and then find "Self-Catering." An E-mail or telephone call will get you the availability information you need.

CHAPTER 8

Gie Her a Haggis!

Eating in Scotland can be an enjoyable adventure for the Independent Golfer. Once you have moved beyond the standard large hotel dining rooms, you enter the world of small, independent restaurants, tearooms, and pubs that offer a delightful variety of fare at reasonable prices. Fish and other seafood are common and delicious in this country, surrounded as it is by the ocean. Game meat – venison, rabbit and grouse – is more common than we would find back home. The venison is a special, low-fat, and tasty treat for the meat eater. There is also the typical fare that is very common to Scots and not too unfamiliar to Americans, though at times, the ways that Scots mix these foods seems a little strange to us. Do you really like a spoonful of baked beans on top of your baked potato?

Breakfast

Scots are proud of their Scottish Cooked Full Breakfast that is served in all Bed and Breakfast establishments and most hotels and restaurants. Just the hearty start-of-the-day meal for the Independent Golfer, it always contains eggs, at least two kinds of breakfast meat, some form of potato, grilled tomatoes, toast or roll, marmalade, coffee and juice and, if you want, porridge (oatmeal) or cold cereal. Different eating establishments vary these basics in a number of ways. Eggs can, of course, be fried, boiled, scrambled, or poached. The breakfast meat could be bacon, which looks like thinly cut and fried strips of ham (regular American-style bacon is cut much thinner and called "streaky bacon" in Scotland). Other meats that are served include veal, pork or beef sausage, black pudding (a kind of black sausage made from minced pork fat, pig's blood, and other ingredients), haggis (more about this later), or kippers (herring that is split, dressed, salted and smoked.) Potatoes come as either a triangular patty of hash browns that has been browned in a skillet or as "tattie scones," thin triangular cakes made from potato flour. Grilled tomatoes, typically two halves warmed facedown in a skillet, are always on your plate. The toast will always be served cool, on purpose. It is presented in a little chrome or silver rack that keeps each slice separate and allows air to circulate freely. Why? Scots say it is to keep the toast crisp. (I always grab it quickly and get butter on it as soon as possible so that the butter will melt before everything goes stone cold. Soggy toast with melted butter is fine to my American palate.) Your Scottish breakfast may also contain sautéed sliced mushrooms and perhaps a spoonful of baked beans.

Though Scots are prideful of their Full Breakfast, they are also aware that not everybody would like such fortification first thing in the morning. You can always ask that some parts of the breakfast not be served. (I never find those baked beans very appetizing in the morning.) You can also opt for a continental breakfast of coffee, juice, and a roll, and you can add yogurt or, at times, fresh fruit.

Lunch

For my Independent Golfing friends, the pub lunch is the most popular way to take a noontime meal. This may be because it is served in a fully-licensed pub that also offers any number of beverages to wash lunch down. But the good food is a great attraction, too. Most pubs will offer a fresh, homemade soup of the day that is hearty, delicious, and inevitably served with a bread roll. Typical soups include scotch broth (an ever-changing combination of meat and vegetables that must always contain barley), lentil, cock-a-leekie (chicken, leeks, and perhaps potatoes), cullen skink (a wholesome combination of smoked haddock, potatoes, onions, spices, and cream), and corn chowder.

Pub lunches offer a variety of other foods, including "toasties" (grilled cheese or ham and cheese sandwiches) and macaroni and cheese. Often you can order baked potatoes or baguettes (French rolls) stuffed with cheese, prawns (small shrimp in a mayonnaise-based sauce), tuna salad, baked beans, or coronation chicken. The latter is a delightful chicken salad that was created for Queen Elizabeth's coronation luncheon in 1953. Along with shredded or chopped chicken, it contains chopped onion, curry paste, tomato puree, red wine, mayonnaise, whipping cream, finely chopped apricots, and salt and pepper.

Fish and chips is a staple of the pub lunch. The fish can be haddock or cod and is typically lightly breaded or battered before frying. It is traditional to sprinkle salt and malt vinegar onto your chips just before you start to eat. The Ploughman's Lunch is more of a light snack lunch than one might think a ploughman would require. It consists of bread and cheese with pickle and a small salad. The construction will vary greatly from pub to pub.

Pub lunches are attractive for a number of reasons. They are typically more inexpensive than comparable fare in larger hotel restaurants. The pubs' informality is appealing to many American visitors who seek to strike up conversations with locals. Pubs, or Public Houses, have, for hundreds of years, been the places that the residents of a local area gather, share news, and discuss the happenings of the day. They are a refuge from work and a haven for the weary who seek to relax with a pint and a friend.

It is this latter, pint thing that, for many, is an extra attraction. The pub lunch always seems to go down better with some libation. The local lager, ale, or any of a number of other brewed beverages are very popular and can be ordered in pint or half-pint glasses. But the Scots don't stop there. Beyond the wide variety of other alcoholic drinks that people around the world are accustomed to, Scots have exercised their imagination in creating additional mixes that are popular locally. You can try a Shandy, which is a half glass of beer filled to the top with lemonade, or try a Lager Tops, which is mostly beer with just a dash of lemonade. If you want to substitute whiskey for that lemonade, you should ask for a Half & Half – whiskey and beer. A whiskey and ginger mix is called a Whiskey Mac. Whiskey mixed with hot water, honey, and lemon is a Toddy and can be very welcome on a blustery day. An interesting mix that is often carried onto the golf course in a flask is Brandy and Port.

When you go to a pub for food or drink, the general custom is to find a place to sit and then walk to the bar, look over a menu and order there. The bartender may ask for the number of the table you will be sitting at, though no number will be visible to you. (Apparently the locals all know the numbers by heart.) Just pointing the table out will be sufficient. You can order your drinks at this time and then carry them to the table. You may be asked to pay before or after being served; the custom varies from pub to pub. When you eat in a pub, you generally serve yourself, though in recent years, some pubs have tended toward hiring servers and moving more toward a restaurant atmosphere.

Scots have a relatively fixed idea about when lunch should be eaten and Americans, wandering into a local pub in a small town at 3:30 in the afternoon will probably be disappointed to find the kitchen closed and nothing available to assuage their hunger but a bag of crisps (potato chips). It is a good idea to plan to eat lunch sometime between noon and 1:30 so that you can both get the best selection the place has to offer and enjoy the atmosphere of a pleasantly crowded pub.

Lunch can also be found in everything from high-end hotel restaurants with elaborate menus, well-set tables, and attentive service to low-end chippies (carry-out fish and chip shops) from which you can walk down the street with a paper box full of your lunch and a bottle of Irn-Bru (a local soft drink so popular it is known as the Scottish national drink). Reasonably sized towns all have small lunch eateries that offer variations of pub lunches, but in a quieter atmosphere that is popular with families and the elderly.

The Independent Golfer will often prefer to eat lunch at the clubhouse on the course after a morning round. The size of the clubhouse is an important factor here. Many of the smaller courses in the Highlands and Islands don't offer regular lunch service. The larger ones offer variations on the pub lunch, but often their selection is somewhat limited. It is quite common for clubs to ask ahead of time for you to book catering (reserve food service) if you want it. In these cases, catering can be simply a snack of coffee and perhaps a bacon roll, or it could be homemade soup and a sandwich. Some clubhouses even offer afternoon High Tea for after your round.

Finally, another option of the Independent Golfer is to buy the makings and fix a picnic lunch. Every reasonably sized town has a market in which you can select from a surprising variety of cheeses that will go well with a freshly baked loaf of bread or crackers. Add some fruit and a bottle of wine and you're set.

Afternoon Tea

Many Scots enjoy afternoon tea, though this custom does not seem as widespread in the north as it is down in England. It really does not seem necessary if you have a good lunch and plan to eat dinner at a reasonable hour. After all, the original Afternoon Tea dates back to the late 1700's, when it was the custom in Britain to eat only two meals a day, breakfast and a rather late dinner. It is said that, complaining of a "sinking feeling" in the late afternoon, the Duchess of Bedford began to take tea and small pastries and then to invite her friends in to share. The custom of afternoon tea was born.

Nowadays most people who indulge do so for the conversation or for an excuse to relax rather than for the need for nutrition, though people who have the habit claim they can't survive the afternoon without it. Tearooms can be found throughout the land and offer both regular tea and High Tea, the difference being what is served with the tea. At the very least, you should get a scone, shortbread or oatcake. As you get "higher," you can expect luxuries like clotted (Devonshire) cream, sweet raspberry jam, crumpets, crustless sandwiches, and assorted pastries, and you will also experience an increased emphasis on presentation – delicate tea cups, silver service, flowers on the table.

Dinner

For dinner in all but the smallest towns, you should have a generous selection of places to eat. It is possible to have pub food for dinner. You can also wander into many types of small independent restaurants as well as restaurants associated with hotels. Most food in these establishments has a considerable Euro-continental flavor, specializing in such things as fish and seafood, beef, lamb and pork, pasta, elaborate salads, and freshly baked breads. Highland Scotch Beef is specially tender and flavorsome, though a bit pricey. In some of the more traditional Scottish places, you will be offered game, meat pies, sausage and mash (mashed potatoes) and, of course, fish and chips. Lamb is always available, but it tends to be quite expensive. (Why this is so I have never understood since, in the Highlands and Islands, you see miles and miles of pastures full of sheep and lambs. Something else must be at work here besides the law of supply and demand.) Deserts are popular with Scots, and you will want to sample the Sticky Toffee Pudding at least once.

Haggis, perhaps the most traditional of Scottish foods, can be found in many restaurants. Haggis has assumed a more exalted state than most Americans might believe that it deserves. This may be, in part, because of the great Scottish poet Robert Burns' "Address to a Haggis" which presumes to tell God how he can best treat Scottish people:

Ye *pow're wha mak mankind your care,*	God
And dish them out their *bill o'fare,*	food
Auld Scotland wants *nae skinking ware,*	no watery food (food with sauces)
That *jaups in luggies,*	splashes in small bowels
But, if you wish her gratefu' pray'r	
Gie her a Haggis!	Give

If you are interested in sampling this dish, be prepared to eat a portion of a large, sausage-like creation made from the chopped heart, lungs and liver of lamb mixed with suet, oats, onions, herbs and spices which, at least traditionally, is packed into a lamb's stomach and boiled. It is, in fact, quite flavorful. Every visitor to Scotland should enjoy this national "treasure" at least once.

Also, if you spend any time in Scotland, you will have to eat chips. What we would call french fries are everyplace and served with everything. Fish and chips, steak pie and chips, sausage and chips, and chicken strips and chips are everywhere. Macaroni and cheese and chips and Lasagna and chips are standard menu items. And then there is just chips. Scots will often buy a stand-alone order of chips for an afternoon or late evening snack. You can order them with curry or tomato-based sauces to dip them in, or enjoy them in the classic way with salt and malt vinegar. Your fine Highland Scot beefsteak at the classiest restaurant will come with chips as will your order of Hungarian Goulash or your lamb shank with mint jelly. Once, when I ordered Kung Pao Chicken and Sweet and Sour Pork at a Chinese take-out place in Tobermory, the young Scot waitress asked with all seriousness, "Do you want chips with that?" I had to ask for rice!

Other Foods

Foreign foods have made a substantial inroad onto the Scottish menu. The British colonial experience in India brought to the UK a wonderfully wide variety of food from the Indo-Pakistani sub-continent that has become so common across the island that it is assumed to be part of British cuisine. Elaborate Indian, Pakistani, Nepalese and Afghanistani restaurants are found in all the major cities of Scotland. Small restaurants and take-out shops are in all but the smallest towns. We found that supermarkets offer a much wider variety of ingredients for such cooking than we ever see in American grocery stores – sauces, curry of all types, many varieties of chutney, breads, and other pastries. This suggests that this cooking is more common in typical Scottish households than one might think. At least, by the number of restaurants, we know that Scots enjoy "eating Indian" when they go out for the evening.

They enjoy other "foreign" foods as well. Chinese restaurants are quite common. Mexican, Caribbean and South American restaurants are appearing, especially in the more tourist-oriented areas where visitors, be they Scots, other British, Europeans or Americans, might be open to taking a fling and trying something different.

An Undeserved Reputation

Scotland, like all of the British Isles, suffers under a reputation for bland food, poorly prepared. At least in Scotland, that is in the past. Though grannies at home might still boil everything, and folks returning from pub crawls might still end their evenings with a stop at the local fish-and-chips shop, the visitor can enjoy a growing variety of cuisine that crosses classic continental fare with local culinary treasurers. Restaurateurs vie for developing new and tasteful ways to present seafood, locally grown "heritage" vegetables and game in appetizing combinations. The higher-end hotels will tempt you to end your meal with an impressive variety of delicious deserts.

Of course, the old beef-and-kidney pie and toasted cheese sandwiches are still available in local pubs for those visitors who want to "eat traditional."

Whatever your choice, finding good food to complement your golf experiences won't be a problem.

CHAPTER 9

Four Seasons in One Day

It was a day full of clouds, huge white billowing ones with dark, rain-laden bases. I was standing on the 14th tee at Strathpeffer Spa in the late afternoon after having slogged through the early part of a round on the lower sections of the course. Mist and drizzle had dissipated in the last 30 minutes to reveal blue patches of sky among the piled clouds. I had managed to keep relatively dry in my rain suit and umbrella and the setting sun was now lighting the hills to the east. Would it be a dry finish after all?

Then I heard an unfamiliar noise, a quiet but persistent "shusshhh" that seemed to be coming from the forest on the side of the hill beyond the 14th green. It grew louder as I listened. My view of the forested hillside began to blur and, as the sound increased, I realized that a strong rain squall had come over the mountain, was bucketing on the hillside a few hundred yards away, and had me in its path.

I grabbed my clubs and dashed to a small grove of pine trees next to the tee, arriving just as the first big drops struck. The pine needles under the trees looked dry. This would be a good place to wait it out. But, to remain completely dry, I unfolded my umbrella and, in order to not have to hold it as I stood, hooked it over two tree limbs above my head. I had a convenient tent under which I could straddle my clubs and avoid the rain that worked its way down through the tree's branches. I wouldn't even have to hold the umbrella. How clever I was! For thirty minutes the rain poured, and for thirty minutes I congratulated myself on being a warm and dry spectator to nature's magnificence.

Then magically, the rain stopped, the clouds cleared in the west, and the setting sun's rays turned my sheltering grove of trees into a palace of diamonds. Thousands upon thousands of droplets, hanging from the tip of every pine needle all about me, danced and sparkled with late afternoon sunlight. I stood in the midst of twinkling, crystalline light, split by each droplet prism into all the rainbow's hues. Then, as I looked outside of my diamond palace to the east, a full and magnificent rainbow appeared in the sky, made all the more brilliant by the almost black clouds that served as its backdrop.

Playing golf in Scotland, you are never far from the weather. It can be awe-inspiring and magnificent, as it was that late afternoon on Strathpeffer Spa. It can be humbling, as the wind often is, especially at seaside courses. Yes, it can be downright miserable as well. Four hours of near horizontal rain can sap the pleasure from any round on even the most magnificent course, especially if the temperature is, as the Scots say, "baltic." And it can change. The locals are fond of saying that Scotland doesn't have a climate, just weather. If you don't like it, just wait a few minutes. It is a national joke that, in Scotland, one can experience four seasons in one day.

The rain on the 14th at Strathpeffer Spa stopped almost as suddenly as it started, and I looked forward to finishing my round warm and dry thanks to the umbrella that I had so cleverly hung above me in the trees. But to get it down, I had to collapse it first. I thumbed the retainer spring and pushed the center pole up above my head. The umbrella collapsed, unleashing what felt like a full gallon of cold rainwater to pour onto my head and down my neck. Who would have dreamed that the outside of an umbrella would retain so much water when it was open, and release it when being shut? I was drenched. I was also cleansed of my prideful arrogance in the face of Scottish weather and reminded, once again, that weather will always be an integral part of golf in Scotland.

Weather can be a challenge in Scotland, but it is not as bad as some would have you think. I have spent countless glorious days on Scottish courses under skies that are equal parts blue and billowy white. The long summer evenings, a blessing of Scotland's high latitude, can be quiet and still, inviting the golfer out to a peaceful round after supper. The moderate breeze that is fairly common, especially on links courses, adds another interesting element that must be factored into your game, along with the slope of the landing area and the break of the green.

What can you expect? Probably the only thing that one can say with certainty about the weather in Scotland is that it is unpredictable. Generally speaking, the west coast of Scotland is wetter but warmer than the east. It benefits from the effects of the gulf stream that wraps around the North Atlantic, bringing warmer currents to lap on western shores. The east is dryer but often receives its weather directly from the North Sea which can add a real nip to the air. This being said, the temperatures across Scotland are never extreme. You never encounter either very hot or very cold conditions. Records show us that the warmest months are July and August, with average highs of 65°. June

Courtesy Golf Highlands

"Brilliant conditions" for golf on Royal Dornoch

averages 63° and September 61°. May and October are 58° and 54° respectively.

For these weather reasons, as well as for reasons related to personal schedules, kids' school holidays and just habit, August seems to be the busiest time of the year for tourists in Scotland, especially the first three weeks, which offer some bank holidays for local Brits and coincide with customary American travel times. June and July are next in the "busiest" line, followed by May and September and then April and October.

Even extreme weather need not be disastrous for your game. Scots regularly play in strong wind, rain or cold, though admittedly, they tend to migrate to the clubhouse when all three are present. The trick is to be prepared for the "conditions" as the Scots call weather changes. The first step in your preparation should be to dress in layers. You can take off your outer shell and sweater as the day warms and then put them back on with a rain jacket over the top when that unexpected squall blows in.

There are a few items that you should always pack along, on even the brightest sunny day. A full-sized golf umbrella is a must. The small, collapsible ones that people carry in the city are only convenient when they are closed up and not in use.

But, because an umbrella becomes difficult to manage in the wind, a good rain hat is also advisable, one with a brim. Some companies now make gortex "rain sombreros" that are lined to keep your head warm and have brims broad enough to keep the rain from running down the back of your neck. I have found that a good hat, along with a good rain suit, is many times more convenient than carrying an umbrella.

A good rain suit is a must. Pants and a rain jacket should be big enough to comfortably fit over your regular golfing ware. I personally think that scrimping on the cost of this part of your equipment is a mistake. Less expensive outfits made of plastic do not "breathe." That is, they make the perspiration that inevitably results from playing golf in any weather accumulate under your outer ware and in your clothing. Then, when finally stripping your rain protection off after the end of a round, you find that you are drenched on the inside, not from the rain but from your own perspiration.

It is a good idea, too, to protect your clubs from a soaking, especially your grips. I find that the club cover that typically comes with a golf bag when it is purchased does not work well. It may initially keep your clubs dry, but only until you try to reach in to get one. Then the cover becomes an awkward barrier to your access that, as you remove it, dumps cups of water into your bag. A number of companies manufacture special bag covers that snap on to the top of your bag, fold over your clubs, and are kept in place by Velcro strips. They give easy access while keeping clubs as dry as possible.

Special rain gloves are a must on very wet days. If the rain continues to fall, no matter what method you use to keep your hands and grips dry, they get wet. And when wet, they slip. More than one golfer with wet grips and little experience in the rain has been surprised to see his club sail off into the rough after slipping from his hands at the end of a swing. A number of companies make special rain gloves, one for each hand, that work quite well in the rain. As advertised, they really do improve the friction of your grip when they get wet. They also serve to keep your hands a little warmer, which might be a welcomed additional advantage on cold days.

A reasonably priced pair of golf shoes that are relatively new and not broken down by unusual abuse are sufficient. Most shoes come from the factory waterproofed. Depending on your care, they can continue to serve well to keep your feet dry for months or even a year or more. But all shoes get wet, even if only on the outside. I always carry two pair with me to ensure that I have a dry pair available at all times.

Preparation is All You Need

You hear many stories about the weather in Scotland, about how fierce it can be and about how it can ruin a golf trip. To be sure, the weather changes, and you might certainly be treated to rain and wind as well as sun and blue skies with puffy white clouds.

The secret is being prepared, and then taking what you are given. Undoubtedly, you will return from Scotland with treasured memories of unsurpassed golf. You may also be lucky enough to have those memories spiced with a little adversity that, itself, will be recalled fondly in years to come.

CHAPTER 10

Featheries, Gutties, and Hickory Shafts

Any book on golf in Scotland will contain a short history about the development of the game. It will relate how historians argue about the game's origins, how it might have been adopted from a game called "het kloven" played on the frozen canals in Holland in which players tried to hit balls into holes in the ice or how it might go back even further to a game named "paganica" played by Romans. It will tell you that golf was so popular in Scotland in the 15th century that King James II had to pass a law discouraging its play because it was interfering with the archery practice of those who would form the King's army when called up. Most histories will delight in pointing out that Mary Queen of Scots was seen to be playing golf in East Lothian rather too soon after the death in 1567 of her second husband Henry Stuart, Lord Darnley, and that James Graham, the Marquis of Montrose was known to have played golf both on the day before and the day after his wedding in 1628.

These histories will then jump forward to the late 18th Century to describe the formation of the early golf clubs, including the Honourable Company of Edinburgh Golfers in 1744, shortly followed by the Society of the St. Andrews Golfers formed in 1754. Finally, the story of the development of early competitions, starting with the first "open" held in Prestwick in 1860, will lead you through the 19th Century and on to modern times.

The difficulty is that such histories contribute little to our understanding of golf as it is now played in Scotland and especially as it is now encountered by the American Independent

Golfer when playing there. We think of Golf as Scotland's game, the game of the people, and it certainly is in this, the opening of the 21st Century. The *2005 Official Guide to Golf in Scotland* lists 546 different courses, which works out to about one course for every 9,000 Scots, including babies and grannies. It is this local popularity that makes golf in Scotland such a wonderful opportunity for Americans. It is as simple as this: Scots love to play golf, they build courses all over the place, they maintain their courses with loving care, and, most important for us, they welcome visitors and appreciate our enjoyment of their game.

But it was not always this way. In the early days, "gowf" developed as a leisurely pursuit for the royalty and their rich friends. The simple fact was that the common folks couldn't afford to play because the equipment was too expensive. First, there was the ball. For almost four centuries until the mid-1800's, golf balls were actually leather spheres stuffed with feathers. Cow- or horse-hide was cut into three sections, softened in alum and water, and then sewn into a sphere using wax thread until only a small gap was left in the seam. The casing was then turned inside out so as to hide the stitches inside the ball.

Stuffing the casing was a difficult and fine art. The ball maker would start with a large pile of feathers, enough, it is said, to fill a gentleman's top hat. The feathers were wet from having been boiled. Though he may have started by pushing a pinch of feathers into the small opening in the leather casing, he soon resorted to using an awl-like tool with a bulbous wooden handle for his palm and a four-inch iron spike that could push one feather at a time into the ball. It was a very laborious and time-intensive task. When all feathers in the top hat were jammed into the small casing and the final stitches were sewn to close it, the ball was hammered into roundness and left to dry. The drying feathers would expand while the drying leather casing contracted, thus producing a surprisingly hard "feathery." With a final coat of paint to protect it from the weather, the ball could be sold to a gentleman golfer for four shillings, a price well beyond the reach of most Scots of the time.

To make the game even more expensive, as you might guess, feathery balls were vulnerable to miss-hits. I picture a golfer hitting his ball thin and watching a cloud of feathers drift away on the wind. Though, in reality, the feathers were too compacted to explode like a pillow, the balls could be damaged easily and, of course, playing on the links among the heather and gorse, these valuable little pellets could be lost as well.

Golf clubs were also works of art and equally expensive. The heads of clubs were made of very tough wood such as apple, beech, holly, or pear and were skillfully connected using a splint, leather straps and string winding to shafts of a more limber or "whippy" wood such as ash or hazel. A gentleman's set of clubs would have consisted of a few play clubs (longnoses) for driving, some fairway clubs (or grassed drivers) for medium range shots, some spoons for short range shots, a niblick or two (similar to today's wedges), and a putting cleek. The cost of such a set would be beyond all but the few wealthiest members of the community.

Clubs were vulnerable too. The ash and hazel shafts were so prone to breaking that it was common for a gentleman golfer to stop by the clubmaker's shop after finishing a round in order to turn in a club or two for repair.

Little wonder that golf before the mid-19th century was a rich man's game. Only the wealthy merchants of the towns and the minor royalty who lived off the produce of the land they held from the King could afford to keep themselves in balls and clubs. Thus, the list of names of the founders of the early golf clubs did not include working men or laborers, farmers or fishermen. As their club names indicate, the founders were Gentlemen Golfers. The only exceptions were the club- and ball-makers themselves, who could make their own equipment and thus be able to enjoy the game. These were, in fact, the first "golf professionals," who had the equipment and the time to perfect their game. Though respected for their playing skill as well as their craftsmanship, these "professionals" were considered by the Gentleman Golfers mere servants.

The Gentleman Golfers of golf's early days were not above saving money wherever they could, and their biggest savings were in the courses they played. The earliest courses were laid out on land owned by the town that was held "in common" for the use of all the town's residents. This common land was generally too poor in quality to be farmed but served as a place to graze stock. Typically near the sea, it could also be used by fishermen to beach their boats for repair, by youths to play games, by archers to practice their war-related skills, and by the general population as a place to take a morning or evening stroll.

As town citizens with access to the town's common land, the Gentleman Golfers could lay out a few holes and play whenever they pleased without paying any use fee to the town. Being men of distinction and power, they were able to persuade other townsfolk to avoid their course layouts. After all, nobody wants to be thumped in the head with a feathery. Sheep and rabbits kept the grass on these courses short and playable. Life for the Gentleman Golfer was good.

Fortunately for us today, all of this changed. As a result of a series of technological developments in the latter half of the 19th Century golf has been "democratized." It has changed from an expensive pastime enjoyed by the privileged few to a game for all Scots and, by extension, for all of us. As a result, courses of fine quality have been created for local play across Scotland and can be enjoyed by the visiting American golfer willing to seek them out.

The first technological development that revolutionized golf was the gutta-percha ball. Gutta-percha is a hard but non-brittle material produced by boiling down the milky sap or latex of the sapodilla tree, most commonly found in Malaysia. Some time around 1848, the Reverend Dr. Robert Adams Paterson received a case of goods shipped to him by a friend in Malaysia. To protect them, these goods were packed in gutta-percha material. The Reverend Doctor found that, if you dip gutta-percha in boiling water, it becomes soft and malleable and can be formed into balls by rolling the softened material on a board.

The result was a wonderfully improved golf ball that was much more durable, resistant to water, went longer off the tee and, most importantly, was much cheaper to make. Even though traditionalists resisted it as a plague that would destroy the game, the "gutty" ball gradually replaced the feathery. By the late 1800's, the cost of golf balls had dropped so that anybody who wanted could take up the game.

It is interesting to note that an early practice with the gutty was to remove any nicks or scratches in the ball after a round of play by boiling and then re-rolling it on a board. As the gutty became more popular, golfers noticed that, if you didn't smooth the ball after use, a many-nicked ball actually had a truer flight than a new or smoothed ball. Golfers began to add an even pattern of marks to their gutties with a sharp edged hammer, thus greatly improving the ball's play. Still later, iron molds or ball presses were used to create patterns of nicks, meshes, lines, and dimples and to revitalize the much-used or damaged balls. "A quick hot bath and a squeeze" was all that was needed to restore a damaged ball to playable condition.

The gutty was replaced at the turn of the century by a rubber ball invented in 1898 by a Cleveland, Ohio golfer named Coburn Haskell. The Haskell ball, which featured rubber thread wound around a solid rubber core, was followed by other innovations in covers, cores, and patternings, all serving to improve ball flight while lowering ball cost.

Club making underwent a similar technological development in the 19th Century. For centuries, club makers had been experimenting with ways to improve the performance of the Gentleman Golfer's clubs. Sizes and shapes of club heads and length of shafts were altered. Different materials, including hardened leather, metal and even bone fragments, were embedded in the club face to improve compression and therefore distance. As early as 1750, forged metal heads appeared, especially as improvements to niblicks. While all of these innovations were intended to improve performance, they also served to push up the cost of clubs, making golf even more inaccessible to the average Scot. In 1826, Robert Forgan introduced the one big change that reduced the cost of clubs when he began using hickory imported from America to manufacture club shafts. Hickory shafts were very durable and not as prone to shattering as were the older ash or hazel ones, and so did not require continued expensive maintenance or replacement. Thus, an initial investment in a set of clubs by an average middle-class golfer could carry him on through many happy days on the links without additional cost.

Two other technological advances in the late 19th century ensured that all Scots who wished to play could enjoy golf. First was the simple mower. Through the 1800's, various farm implements were created to mechanize and enhance the various tasks that farmers performed. One of these was a set of revolving blades carried on a set of wheels that could be pulled behind a team of horses to cut grass which could then be fed to livestock. In 1890, an enterprising golfer realized that such a mower could be used to cut fairways in grassy fields and meadows in the rolling farmland of Scotland. Before this time, golf was only played on links land where the grasses indigenous to this ocean-side environment could be cropped by sheep and rabbits into ideal fairways and greens. The mower allowed golf courses to be built in other landscapes.

The Gentleman Golfers in the old established clubs were the first to latch onto this new idea. The growing popularity of golf had led to all sorts of common folk showing up on the common lands of seaside cities and towns like Leith, Musselboro and St. Andrews with their gutties and hickory-shafted clubs eager to play. After all, it was common land. They had a right to play there, too. Faced with this invasion of the "lower classes", the Gentlemen Golfers moved their play to new sites, typically in the foothills of the Highlands where they could fence off, for their own private use, the fairways and greens that they could create with the new mowers. Private clubs, often associated with expensive hotels, were created that offered the well-heeled visitor golf, fishing, and hunting adventures, all safely located away from the masses.

The other technological innovation that contributed to the democratizing of golf was the railroad. As the growing middle class in Great Britain was enjoying increased prosperity, the need grew for ways to spend their accumulating income on enjoying life. Taking vacations to remote places in the Highlands of Scotland came into vogue. If the very rich could have their lodges and hotels, so too could the middle class. The railroads were just the thing to enable a middle-class family to travel relatively quickly to the country. With this rapid travel, a week or two of vacation was possible in the north. Railroad spur lines were built to any number of resorts and spas that grew up in the Scottish north. These lines carried growing numbers of vacationers from the cities to enjoy golf at their leisure. Many small communities built their own courses, both as places for the locals to play and as a way to attract additional income into areas that were otherwise struggling economically.

Through the first part of the 20th century, a wonderful string of courses across the Highlands and Islands came into being. Most were founded in the period between 1885 and 1915. (Today the current golfing boom is spurring construction of new courses, especially in areas that are tourist destinations.) Some of the old courses are classic golfing venues whose reputations continue to attract visitors from all over the world. Others offer delightful golfing challenges but are little known beyond their own region. All are lovingly maintained and administered by local Scots who could not conceive of a life without their beloved game. All exist because golf grew from the pastime of the elite to become Scotland's game, a game for everyone.

CHAPTER 11

Scotland Beyond the Courses

As we peeked out of the dormer window of our B&B in Fort Augustus, our fears were justified. The skies were gray. It looked like rain. The BBC weather report on the television described a band of heavy squalls to the north of us over the Moray Firth and Dornoch, exactly where my three buddies, Ben, Nick, and Orin, and I were headed for a week of golf. It didn't look like there would be much golf this day. We had a tee time at Royal Dornoch at 1:00 that was a definite washout. It would take a two hour car ride to travel there, and we had a whole day to do it in. What were we to do?

Over breakfast, the local skies cleared to reveal patches of blue sky among clouds that were at times white and puffy but at other times dark and heavy with rain. We might have played locally, but we chanced into another possibility for passing time: attend the local Highland Games!

The night before, my traveling buddies and I had been lucky to find four seats in a local pub in Fort Augustus that was chock-a-block (full up) with local Scots. It didn't take us too long to learn that most of these pub-goers were in town for the Fort Augustus Highland Games, a much-anticipated local event that draws participants and spectators from all over the central Highlands. Beers in hand, a number of locals filled us in on what to expect. Pipe bands were coming from all over the country to march and play. Dancers would compete in offering their versions of traditional Scottish Highland dances. There would be a sheep dog exhibition and a demonstration of falconry.

But for most in the pub, the central attraction would be the competition of the "heavies," that is, athletes who would compete in a variety of strength events. There would be three contests for distance. The Clachneart (Stone) Toss is very similar to a modern shot-put, except the shot is not an iron ball but a stone weighing 16 pounds. In the Weight Toss, the athlete spins about in a circle on the ground and then throws a 56-pound weight for distance. In the Hammer Throw the athlete also spins about, but this time holding to the end of a four-foot long wooden handle with a 16 pound weight attached to it as the hammer head. After a few spins he launches it into the air, hoping that it sails in the right direction. The spectators ringing the field share his hope.

They would have the Weight Toss for Height in which the athlete swings a 56-pound weight between his knees and then tosses it up over a bar above his head which can vary in height much like a pole vaulter's bar. Because the bar is straight above the athlete's head, the trick is to launch the weight up as high as you can and then get out of the way before it comes back down. There would be a Sheaf Toss, in which an athlete uses a pitch fork to toss a sheaf of hay wrapped in burlap and weighing between 15 and 25 pounds over a bar. The guy that tosses it over the highest bar wins.

And then, of course, there is the most popular Caber Toss, a contest that delicately balances strength with coordination and accuracy. A caber is an 18-foot long log that weighs between 100 and 120 pounds. Holding one end the athlete first balances the caber as it juts straight up in the air. He then tosses it so that it flips end over end once, lands with the top of the caber hitting the ground and then falls away from him so that it lies on the ground with the end that the athlete was holding pointing directly away from him. The athlete with the straightest toss is the winner. Distance has no bearing on the outcome.

This all sounded great to us the previous night and, seeing local sunshine (at least partial) and hearing a forecast of rain at our destination, we decided over breakfast to stay in Fort Augustus and see the Games. (Independent Golfers can do this. We didn't have a bus schedule to meet or other tour participants to consult.) Driving to the edge of town, we parked among some trees and walked down a dirt road about 100 yards to an open field ringed by tents and trucks. We gave up searching for a booth to buy admission tickets when Ben finally convinced the rest of us that admission was free. (Why do we find it so difficult to jettison the idea that we have to pay for everything?) We joined a throng of folks strolling along the line of tents that circled the field. Like a small town weekend sidewalk sale back home, these tented vendors had all sorts of things for sale: jewelry, books, clothing, music CD's, candy, hot dogs (yes, hot dogs with mustard but no pickle relish), beer, and soft drinks. We stopped in front of a falconry club's travel trailer and looked over eight beautiful birds of prey that sat on short perches arranged in a ring. Two Harris Hawks, a European Sparrowhawk, a Peregrine Falcon, a Great Horned Eagle, two Barn Owls and a gorgeous White Owl all sat calmly and watched us watch them.

The sheepdog demonstration was in full swing as we arrived. The handler, appropriately decked out in his kilt as were many of the spectators, showed off his dog's talents herding a group of geese, not sheep. The dog didn't care what she worked. She was all ears to her handler's voice as he shouted short commands and she moved the squawking geese about the field, at last herding them into a three-sided pen and sitting guard, waiting for one to chance an escape.

Then came the marching bands, drums and bagpipes thrumming and skrilling traditional pipe music. Most remarkable about these bands was their cross-generational and cross-gender nature. Beautiful teenaged girls stood proud and tall next to elderly men. School boys and their mothers played side by side. This was a hobby for them. There is no money to be made in dressing up in full kilt and sporran (the fury bag that hangs from the waist in front of the kilt), white shirt with lace trim and jacket with all the adornments and marching around a grassy field. They clearly do it for the love of their art and for the tradition that connects them to their proud past.

In all, it was a memorable morning. The athletes did their best to out-toss each other. The eagle soared overhead but returned to the bait that the falconer twirled about his head on the end of a leather thong. The girls danced their traditional dances and, though they all looked the same to us, one pair walked away with the blue ribbon. The Master of Ceremonies coaxed three young women into competing in the hammer throw, but they giggled so much that they could hardly lift the thing, let alone throw it. Standing so near to the "heavies" was apparently too much for them. We left in the early afternoon after a lunch of hot dogs and beer and had plenty of time to complete the drive to Dornoch. Such is the life of the Independent Golfer in Scotland.

When my three buddies and I go to Scotland, we go to play golf. Typically we play 36 holes a day, almost always at the same course, morning and afternoon. After a morning round and a good lunch in the clubhouse or a nearby pub, we return for an afternoon eighteen. We have found that playing two rounds on the same course has its advantages. We always hope that the afternoon will bring us better scores, benefiting as we think we do from the "local knowledge" that we presumably accumulated in the morning and the beverages that we consumed at lunch. Two rounds at the same course also saves money. Almost all courses will sell you a "day pass" for less than the cost of two separate rounds. We Independent Golfers are always looking for a less expensive way to do things.

Though golf generally fills most of our time on these trips, we have found it enjoyable to take some time out now and then to seek out other interesting things that Scotland has to offer. I have also taken golf trips to Scotland with folks who do not play. My wife is not a golfer and, on occasion, golfing friends have companions who do not play. For these folks, it is especially important to note the wide and wonderful variety of diversions that the visitor can find in Scotland. The Highland Games that day in Fort Augustus was just one pleasant example of "Scotland beyond the golf courses" that an Independent Golfer should be aware of.

History

Scotland's landscape is crowded with the relics, artifacts, and sites of its long and rich history. The remains of Neolithic and Iron Age settlements compete for your attention with medieval castles, battlefields, stately country homes, workplaces from the early industrial revolution, and remains of World War II installations. Local tourist bureaus are well stocked with advice and pamphlets about their nearby historical sites of interest, but a few must be mentioned here.

Castles are everywhere in the Scottish North. Much of Scottish history revolves around bloody feuds between rival Highland clans or outright war with the English to avoid subjugation or regain independence. In such a violent land, everybody had to live under the protection of warlords who themselves created strong fortresses as bases from which to operate. As you travel through Scotland, you will repeatedly come across the ruins of these fortresses, perched on rocky hills or on islands in lakes or along the seacoast. Most are tumbled-down piles of rock with a few partial walls still standing. They might be a few minutes walk from the nearest road and, though guarded by signs that warn of the danger if you climb over them, they are open to casual exploration. A few castles which were notable by their size or important role in history have been partially restored and are administered by the National Historical Trust. At castles like Urquhart on Loch Ness in the Great Glen (nearby golf courses are Inverness, Loch Ness and Torvean) or Eileen Donan near the Kyle of Lochalsh (nearby courses include Isle of Skye, Gairloch, Traigh), you can see interpretative displays of castle life, watch movies about local history, and walk through low doorways into the great halls or up the winding stairways onto the walls and parapets that defined the castle's defenses.

Through the last few centuries, many castles evolved from purely defensive fortresses to become stately country homes of the landed nobility. A fine example of this is Dunrobin, the most northerly and one of the most majestic of Scotland's great houses. (Nearby golf courses are Royal Dornoch, Brora, Tain, and Golspie) Located 50 miles north of Inverness on the North Sea coast, it is one of Britain's oldest continuously inhabited houses, dating in part from the early 1300's. It is the seat of the Sutherland family which includes previous Earls and Dukes and the current owner who is a Countess and who allows a few of Dunrobin's 189 rooms to be viewed by the public. A tour of Dunrobin features great halls with fine furniture, family portraits, and a lavish and extensive formal garden in which falconry exhibits are offered every afternoon.

Unfortunately, the Sutherlands are best known in Scottish history not for having the largest house in the Highlands but for their role in the Highland Clearances. In the late 1700's and early 1800's Highland landowners evicted thousands of peasant farmers whose families had been renting the lands they farmed for generations. Why? The landowners thought they could make more money raising sheep. Just a few shepherds could tend thousands of sheep on the land that had been worked by hundreds of farming families. Less labor, more profit for the landowner. But this "progress" came at great pain and hardship to the local farmers who were forced by the police or the army to leave their homes to make room for the sheep. Many of the worst atrocities seen during the Highland Clearances were committed on Sutherland lands. Families were literally turned out without notice into the winter cold and snow. Their houses were burned, at times with the elderly or infirmed still inside. The people could only take away what they could carry on their backs, and they often had no place to go. Many ended as factory workers in the slums of cities like Glasgow, or they migrated by the thousands to Canada, Australia, or the United States. The Clearances are a dark chapter in Scottish history, and their effects are still felt in the contentious nature of current land laws and experiments in land diversification schemes being pursued today.

Enjoying the Out-Of-Doors

It may seem a little silly to talk about walking, cycling, horseback riding and canoeing as an alternative activity on a golfing vacation in Scotland, but there are two things that make it worth mentioning. First, there may be somebody along on the holiday who isn't keen to play golf every day and who would enjoy spending time in the wonderful outdoors of the Highlands and Islands. Hiking, or as the Scots refer to it "hill-walking," is a popular pastime in the North. Almost every region has a local hill-walking group that has set out trails through glens, across moorlands and mountains and along beaches. These trails are clearly marked, graded as to difficulty and labeled with the time it would typically take to complete them. Some are just casual walks along bubbling creeks in old-growth forests. Others are more strenuous and lead to the top of mountain peaks with the reward of fabulous views.

Hill-walking and other outdoor activities are typically found in a few "centers" in the Highlands, and, fortunately, these places generally feature great opportunities for golf as well. One such center is the village of Gairloch on the West coast north of the Isle of Skye. The area has been a popular holiday resort since Victorian times, when visitors came in on regular steamships from the south. In those days, most visitors put up at the Gairloch Hotel, but today's visitors have a wide choice of accommodation. For recreation, you can walk, rock climb, sail, fish, water ski, windsurf, canoe/kayak, and pony trek. In the summer, the local inns and hotels frequently hold ceilidhs (see below) and musical evenings. And, of course, there is the delightful Gairloch Golf Club that, within its nine holes, offers a substantial range of golf challenges.

The 8th tee and fairway "Traigh Mor" at Gairloch Golf Club are the beginning of a demanding par-5 that offers trouble left and right and hides the green in front of the white clubhouse in the distance.

The #7 "An Dun" asks you to hit a delicate 88-yard blind shot from a tee box that hangs on the wooded hillside over a heather-covered hill that hides both the triangular green and the two bunkers that guard the back left and right. This subtle hole is followed by Gairlock's demanding par-5 #8 "Traigh Mor." Off the tee, you must hit into a 25-yard wide landing area placed on the spine of a ridge. Death on the left takes the form of a grass-covered cliff, a beautifully curving sandy beach, and OB. The right is little better, a steep rough-covered hillside. A good tee shot in the fairway and a bold feeling encourages the golfer, on the second swing, to carry the brow of the hill up which the fairway runs. Success leads to a pitch to the green and a possible birdie. The less bold endeavor moves the golfer only part-way up the hill, thus offering a long but clear third shot to the green. After those early swings, all else is simple.

Ownership of land, and restrictions on its use by its owners, has been a difficult issue in Scotland for hundreds of years.

Systems of land ownership that grew out of feudal times and that persisted into the modern era put most of the country under the control of a very few landed aristocrats. In the 1890's, the Duke of Sutherland, landlord to most of the Scottish Northern Highlands, was the largest landowner in all of Europe! Though not using it themselves, the landowners' often restricted access to others. That is all changing now with the Scottish Parliament's passage in 2003 of the Scottish Land Reform Act. Under this Act, people can gain non-motorized access over most land and inland water for activities such as walking, cycling, horseback riding, and canoeing as long as they do so responsibly. Though the Scots are in the midst of implementing this far-reaching reform, it bodes well for the common folks, as they seek to enjoy the beautiful land in which they live. And, of course, it holds great possibilities for Independent Golfers who are looking for outdoors recreation off the course.

Battlefields

With such a bloody history, the small country of Scotland could be expected to be dotted with sites of battles and skirmishes among local clans and between them and their ever-encroaching English neighbors. There is Glen Coe (nearby courses include Dragon's Tooth and Fort William) where, in 1692, some Campbells, who had been invited into the houses of local MacDonald residents for the night, rose up at 5 a.m. and attacked their hosts in their beds, massacring thirty-eight MacDonalds and driving many more out into the snow to die.

The one battlefield that stands out from all the others is Culloden Moor, the site of arguably the most important battle fought in Scottish history. (Nearby courses are Inverness, Loch Ness, Muir of Ord, Nairn and Nairn Dunbar.) In 1745, Charles Edward Stuart, known as Bonnie Prince Charlie, led an uprising intending to throw the English rulers out of Scotland and restore his father, James VIII, to the Scottish throne. King George II of England sent his son, the Duke of Cumberland, north to put down what the English saw as a rebellion. Armed with the latest artillery, Cumberland's army met Charlie's Highlanders on Culloden Moor on a cold drizzly day in April, 1746. Charlie's highland men, who carried their great broadswords, the claymores, were no match for Cumberland's redcoats and their artillery. The battle lasted less than an hour, but it was the battle's aftermath that had such terrible consequences for Scotland and that are felt even today. In the hours after the battle, following the orders of Cumberland to "give no quarter," the redcoats scoured the battlefield, methodically killing all the wounded they could find. Cumberland, who earned the nickname that day of "The Bloody Butcher," sent his cavalry in pursuit of Charlie's fleeing men, killing all they could find. The killing, that went on for days, was just the beginning. In the following weeks and months, government redcoats swept through the Highlands in a reign of terror, officially searching for rebels but in reality murdering, raping, and pillaging all they could find. The land was stripped of all its wealth and resources in the hopes that the inhabitants would starve and freeze.

Highland chiefs were killed and their land declared forfeit to the king. The system of law that had governed the Highlands for centuries was abolished. The carrying of arms was outlawed, as was even the mention of Charlie's name. Likewise, the wearing of kilts or any clothing made of plaid or tartan and even the playing of the bagpipes were made illegal. Breaking of any of these bans was punishable by death. The highlanders suffered a true "ethnic cleansing" after Culloden that systematically stripped them of their culture and their heritage. When it was over, the Highland clan system was gone forever. Thousands fled their land to the American colonies and Nova Scotia in Canada. Those who remained struggled for generations to regain their culture and self-respect, a struggle that still goes on in the minds of many Scots today.

Whiskey

    One Scottish cultural tradition that was happily not obliterated after Culloden is the making of whiskey. Tradition says that the Scotti brought whiskey-making to Scotland from Ireland in the 5th century. Judging by the fact that there are now over 140 different whiskey distilleries in the country, one must think that this had to be one of the most successful "invasions" that this land has experienced.

In Raphaell Holinshead's *Chronicles*, published in 1564, the author writes of the value of whiskey to the Scots: "Being moderately taken it cutteth fleume, it lighteneth the mynd, it quickeneth the spirits, it cureth the hydrpsie, it pounceth the stone, it repelleth the gravel, it puffeth away ventosite, it kepyth and preserveth the eys from dazelying, the tongue from lispying, the teeth from chattering, the throte from rattyling, the weasan from stieflying, the stomach from womblying, the harte from swelling, the belie from wirthching, the guts from rumblying, the hands from shivering, the sinews from shrinkying, the veynes from crumplying, the bones from akying, the marrow from soakying, and truly it is a sovereign liquor, if it be orderlie taken." Holinshead says nothing about whiskey "kepything the ball from slicing" but I'm sure that many a Scot would testify to such additional efficacious qualities of the "bog water."

Distillery visits are now considered by many an essential part of any golfing holiday in the Highlands and Islands. You can learn about the surprising variety of single malt whiskeys, the processes by which they are made, the differences between the single malts and the blends, and the qualities that make each whiskey unique. Many distilleries have beautifully decorated visitor centers equipped with gift shops and tasting rooms. Some also have tea rooms, restaurants, museums, and even film theatres. All are staffed with friendly and informative greeters and guides eager to explain why their distillery's whiskey is just a bit better than their competitor's in the next glen over. They will invite you to sample a dram of their product – or perhaps two or three – and then to buy if you wish.

The reasons given by each distillery as to why it is able to produce a whiskey that is better than any of the others are varied and, at times, imaginative. They all use the same basic distilling process: Barley is malted by steeping it in water for two to three days, causing the seed-heads to sprout. The malted barley is then dried over a slow fire, milled into a grist, and mixed with hot water. The sweet liquid is then mixed with yeast in a large vat and allowed to ferment for about two days. The alcoholic solution that results from this fermenting process is then distilled in a spirit still. The output of the sill is put into oak casks for maturing, a process that takes at least eight years and perhaps even twenty or thirty to produce good whiskey.

So, why are whiskeys so different? The distinctive character of any distillery's product is said to be the result of the water that flows through the particular glen where the distillery is located, the barley they use and how they grind it, the types of yeast used, or the particular type and origin of the peat that is burned when drying the malt. They also speak of the way the vats and stills are emptied and filled, the size and shape of the stills, the type of casks in which the whiskey matures, the environment of the warehouse in which the casks lie, the time that is given to the maturing process, and even the micro-climate that the distillery enjoys.

What's the best combination? With over 140 different distilleries, each producing a different product, it will be up to you to decide. Some are light and fragrant of flowers or fruit, some sweet but with a dryish finish, some spicy or smoky with a distinct peaty flavor, and some full flavored, rich, and even medicinal in nature with notes of iodine, carbolic or creosote. They are all meant to satisfy individual tastes, and the whiskey connoisseur's goal must be to try them all. How else can one find one's favorite?

The tasting of whiskey is, itself, done differently in Scotland than in America. The Scots don't use ice, soda, or other mix, just straight up at room temperature. But the shot is served in a larger glass, and you will notice on the bar small pitchers of water. Each individual, to his own taste, may add a bit of water to the glass to "dampen the fire" of the alcohol and allow the flavors of the whiskey to "open." Some say a teaspoon of water is enough; any more will "drown" the whiskey. Others mix as much as half-and-half whiskey and water. Still others don't use water at all and consider those who do silly. The mix is up to the drinker, not the barkeep.

Local Music

Some pubs and clubs in the larger towns and cities may feature local musicians who offer an evening's entertainment. Happily, the imported rock, pop, and disco craze is subsiding in Scotland in favor of traditional music or its modernized versions.

One evening, my wife and I offered to take our two daughters to see the Peat Bog Faeries. The girls are both in their early twenties and were visiting us for a week in Inverness. "The who?" they squawked incredulously, "A group called the Peat Bog Faeries? You have got to be kidding!" "No, no, no, they're good. You'll like them," we pleaded as we dragged these reluctant American kids into The Hootenanny, a local folk club in downtown Inverness. My wife and I snagged two beers and the last couple of seats as the room filled with happy Scots. It was clear that the fire marshal wasn't expected this night, as people continued to pour in, jamming themselves behind posts and on the tops of booths until those few of us who had been lucky enough to find seats were surrounded with a forest of bodies, all downing beers and loudly talking with friends. Most were in their twenties or thirties, but there were enough mature adults to make my wife and I feel not completely out of place.

As our daughters watched with growing fascination, the band members, concluded conversations with their friends, casually separated from the crowd and assembled on the slightly raised stage in the bay window at the front of the room and readied their instruments to play. At first glance, they could have been any modern rock group: guys in their twenties playing lead guitar, bass, electronic keyboards and drums. But then there was the violin player and the piper with his bagpipes. And there was their clothing – kilts and T-shirts with work boots and knee-high socks drooping down around the ankles in a manner apparently taken by them to be very stylish.

And then they started playing. It was a wild combination of rapid-fire 16th notes on the pipes and fiddle backed by a thrumbing bass line, keyboard riffs, and a driving rhythm from the drums. The melody was an old jig from their Scottish past. The delivery was as complex and energetic as only very contemporary music can be. The room throbbed, and people started moving. They grinned, they swayed, they waved their arms in the air and danced. I couldn't sit still. The rhythm that first infected my left foot causing it to tap the floor spread up my leg and across my whole body so that, before I knew it, I was bouncing and moving in my seat. And then I realized that I was the only person in the room still sitting. Everyone else had discarded their chairs, which had been thrown into the corner in order to make more room to dance. We weren't on a dance floor, we were in a dance room. Everybody, from wall to wall, was moving.

The Faeries continued to play one tune after another, without a break, for two hours. Occasionally they would change the pace and offer a haunting melodious aire for which the piper would exchange his bagpipes for a whistle and the fiddle would keen. Then back to a foot-stomping reel to the shouted joy of the crowded room.

Our daughters were captivated by the music and its energy. They danced the night away, laughing at each other and savoring the unfettered joy of this modernized Celtic music. When the evening ended, they clamored to buy the Faeries two music CD's and talked to band members about the possibility of touring in the States. When I asked later what my younger daughter had to say about being so taken with a boy who wears a dress and plays a violin, she only had a smile.

There is a difficulty in finding these kinds of happenings. VisitScotland places don't typically feature information about entertainment intended for local people, and so a traveler might never be aware of the possibilities. Locals have a way of discovering these events without benefit of large advertising campaigns. Talking to people is the best bet, or looking for fliers printed on 8 1/2 x 11 paper stock taped into the windows of local stores.

My wife noticed such a flyer one day in the window of the local market in Dornoch. It advertised a Ceilidh (pronounced KAY-lee, believe it or not) to be held on the coming Saturday night to benefit the Sutherland Pipe Band from Golspie that wanted to go on a tour to Calgary, Canada, the following year. A Ceilidh is a wonderful form of evening entertainment that has survived in Scotland from the time before television or even movies. A band, which plays classic country Scottish dance music, typically includes a "caller" who calls out directions to the set dance moves. Clearly precursors to our American square dances, these Scottish country dances form couples into groups of eight dancers and ask them to step around the floor, turn around each other, weave in and out, and link arms and spin, all to lively fiddle, accordion, and drum music. Waltzes, jigs, reels and two-steps alternate. Everybody dances.

In a typical ceilidh, after a few dances a Master of Ceremonies will interrupt the music to invite some individuals to come up to offer an entertainment. That person might sing a solo, perhaps accompanied by a piano player, or recite a poem. The evening alternates between country dancing and these individual offerings.

The fact that the Sutherland Pipe Band's ceilidh was to be held at Dunrobin Castle (see its description above) was not the only reason Susan and I decided to attend, but it certainly didn't hurt. It is a rare opportunity to be able to get into Dunrobin at night.

Our evening was thoroughly enjoyable, though we were obviously the only non-locals among the 100 or so attendees. The admission was modest, £5 ($8.50), as was the dress of the other dancers, which happily allowed us to blend in with our limited traveling wardrobe. I bought two tickets for £1 each to the raffle at the door. Why not help the pipe band get to Calgary?

The castle's grand ballroom was lit with candles, its walls lined with great portraits of Sutherlands back through the centuries. The furniture was pushed back to make room on the polished wooden floor for the dancing. As we found two seats on the side of the room, the band started playing and my wife, eager participant that she is, dragged me onto the dance floor. We had no idea what we were doing, which was, of course, very obvious to everybody in the room. Following a dance caller's directions, if you have never done the dance before, is hard enough. Following a caller with a thick Scottish accent is, at least for me, pretty impossible. But the other couples in our group joined in, pushed us here, moved us there, spun us around when appropriate, and generally guided us through the dance with eager enthusiasm. Not put off by our foreign intrusion into their evening, these folks were happy to see us try their dances and keen to have us succeed.

The entertainments this evening were all old Scottish songs, mostly offered by rather elderly but very distinguished gentlemen or ladies who stood properly in front of the band as they intoned their offerings. The Sutherland Pipe Band also marched in, filling the room with the sound of its pipes and drums. Most in the Band were high school students, though some may have been recently graduated to join the local workforce. They were all dressed sharply in their kilts, tunics, knee socks, and bonnets and were clearly very proud to be performing for us.

A highlight of the evening was the raffle. Mothers of the band members had clearly shaken down a number of local merchants, and the prizes were numerous. Bottles of wine or whiskey, dinners for two in local restaurants, and gift certificates in local stores predominated. One mother circulated among the seated guests with the ticket basket, asking different individuals to close their eyes and pull out the next winning ticket. Each announcement of a winner was followed by polite applause and, if the prize was wine or whiskey, an amusing remark about putting it to good use. Then, with a healthy gift certificate of £25 in a Scottish apparel shop in Inverness was offered, they called my wife's number. A ruffle of whispers followed by hearty applause filled the room. Yes, she is the winner, the American. Everybody was clearly pleased that Susan, a stranger, had won. During a time for tea and cookies later in the evening, any number of people approached her, inquiring about how she would spend the gift. On a kilt for her husband? No? Maybe a sweater for herself. Yes, that would do.

CHAPTER 12

Mina Berrn

My first opportunity to play golf in Scotland was on the Old Course at St. Andrews some 30 years ago. I arrived as a single and was fortunate to be put with three local Scots for the round. Though understandably nervous on the first tee of the most famous course in the world, I managed to hit a decent drive into the fairway. (If you know the Old Course, you'll know that hitting the first fairway isn't a great accomplishment. It is almost as wide as it is long.) Still, the green was a relatively short iron away, and I was feeling good.

As I prepared to hit my second shot, one of my Scottish playing partners called over from about 30 yards away, "Mina berrn." Having no idea what he meant, I cocked an ear and gestured for him to repeat himself. "Mina berrn!" he called a bit louder. Still not understanding, but not wanting to appear too dense, I smiled, nodded, and waved. I then turned to my ball and struck it as well as I could hope to. It sailed up and out, straight in line to the pin. I was ecstatic. As it dropped toward the green, I expected to see it hit, bounce, and run up to the hole. Instead, it disappeared!

What? My ball was there, tracking toward glory one moment and gone the next. I couldn't imagine what had happened until I walked forward, close enough to see a small stream winding across the fairway just at the front edge of the green, the Swilkin Burn. (The Scots call streams "burns".) From where I had hit my shot, that burn had been invisible. The fairway appeared to be perfectly unblemished as it rolled up to the green. But no ball was going to run onto that green. The wary golfer had to hit his second shot so that it carried the burn, minding that he didn't come up a bit short and in trouble. I hadn't minded the burn, and I paid the price.

I learned at least three things that day. First, I learned that Scots are generally wonderful people to play golf with. They take their game seriously but enjoy the success of others as well as their own and are eager to help a fellow golfer succeed. Mind you, you will never hear a Scot volunteer advice as to things like stance, grip, or swing, especially on the course. The tendency in Scotland is to think of the swing as a whole anyway, and Scots typically are less interested in swing mechanics and analysis. What you will hear is endless conversation about the course, how it plays, peculiar characteristics of individual holes and how others, especially famous pros or golfing personalities, played particular holes with more or less success in the past. They are quite willing to share secrets of the course, the good line off the tee, the way a green accepts an approach shot, or a hidden break in the green that all the locals know about.

The second thing I learned is that Scots are often hard to understand. True, they all speak English, but some regional accents are almost beyond American comprehension. Just try to get directions from a truck driver in Glasgow some time. Still, perhaps because they tend to be such a good-natured people anyway, it is perfectly fine to smile, admit you don't understand, and ask for things to be repeated. People really don't mind.

The third thing I learned on the first hole at St. Andrews, and the thing that is important for the present discussion, is that Scotland's golf courses are subtle and, at times, even devious. Things are not always as they appear. It is common for holes to be designed with burns that cross the fairway just at the places where well-struck balls might land. And, as with the first hole at St. Andrews, these burns are often hidden from the view of the unwary or the uninitiated. Bunkers are not only placed where tee shots or approach shots that are a bit off line might reach, they are often hidden from view. From the tee box, you might look out to see one bunker on the left of the fairway near the turn of the dogleg, but only 150 yards away. Knowing that you can carry that little bunker, you are tempted to cut the dogleg and gain perhaps 30 yards toward the pin. The difficulty is that you don't see the line of four other bunkers stringing out beyond the one in view, each more eager than the other to gather in your drive.

This subtle quality of many Scottish courses can be quite devious. As you come up to a hole for the first time, you might see a broad fairway with little apparent difficulty. Why, then, did the ball that you hit just to the right of center kick and then run in a great arc to the right until it stopped in a patch of gorse that seemed well out of play before you hit? Why did the ball you hit directly at the pin run left all the way across the green, giving you a 40-foot putt instead of the 8-footer you expected?

Not all of these hidden "forces" on Scottish courses result in heartache. That seemingly broad and benign fairway that took your ball unexpectedly right to trouble? Know enough to hit your tee shot down a line just to the left instead of the right of center, and you will delight in seeing your ball bound on, dip out of sight for a moment in a swale, and then reemerge still running toward the green. Know enough to hit your approach shot toward a "bail-out" area to the right of the blind green, and you will be rewarded as you walk over the hill to see that your ball will have run down off the apron, across the green, and be resting happily, five feet from a birdie.

This is all, of course, "local knowledge." These are things that people come to know about their courses after playing them for years. We Americans all have things that we know about our own local courses that strangers would benefit from, but the Scottish courses seem to have more of this. The great course architects of the past who were responsible for most of the wonderful Scottish courses seem to have delighted in setting up their tracts with hidden rewards and punishments. From Old Tom Morris to James Braid and Donald Ross, these giants knew that the subtle nuances of the course are what give it its challenge and character.

When playing golf in Scotland, there is also the much more basic need to know distances. How far is that fairway bunker off the tee? How far is it from this patch of heather to the center of the green? How deep is the green? Is the pin cut on the front, middle, or back? That is to say, knowing distances is a basic need of Americans. But it is not a Scottish need. We are accustomed to distance aids, a lot of them. Our American courses all have 100, 150, 200, and where needed, 250 yard markers embedded in the fairways. Each course has some system for telling the approaching golfer where the pin is located today: front, center, or back.

Scots tend much more to play by eye, and by feel. They ask, how important is it to know that you are 165 yards from the green when you are hitting downhill, into a 25-mile per hour wind, and know that the fairway in front of this green will allow your ball to run well past where it lands? In what appears to be a concession to American style, many Scottish courses have placed some sort of distance marker on each hole, but probably just one, and different courses use different systems. One course might use a blue disk placed in the middle of the fairway 125 yards from the green's center. Another might put a white pole at the side of the fairway 150 yards from the green's front edge. Most Scot players might note these distance aids on occasion. But just as likely, they will continue to play by feel, especially if they know the course and are playing in windy conditions. Very few Scottish courses have any system for telegraphing pin placement – front, center or back. Scots learn to eye placements as they pass greens that they will play later in the round.

An experienced caddie can help you understand the particularities of a course. They can tell you something about distance, though it likely will be expressed as "Hit your seven" rather than in terms of yards to carry. Access to such information might cut three or four strokes off of your score. (I say "might" because it is one thing to know what line and distance to hit your ball. It is another thing to do it.) If you want to avail yourself of this help, caddies are available on many of the larger Scottish courses, though, quite frankly, their quality varies widely. Some great old guys are still around who are very good players themselves, have bagged around the course for 40 years, and know everything about it. But you might also draw a youngster looking for extra money who is basically a bag carrier.

On the other hand, you way wish to tackle a new course on your own, trusting your eye to steer you around. I must admit that I enjoy this approach myself, looking at it as a game of discovering the ways to best navigate the course and uncovering the secrets that the course hides from the less perceptive. Many of the larger courses are now publishing "stroke savers," small booklets that present diagrams of each hole with hazards and distances clearly marked. If you need to know distances, these can surely help. But they tell you nothing about how the fairways will carry your drives, which sides are best for approaching greens, and how greens might accept approach shots hit to their different areas. You will still need to use your eye for much of your navigation.

Even with the best intentions and efforts, things can go drastically wrong. There is no worse feeling than to hit what you think is a great drive, only to see it run on through the fairway at the dogleg and into the rough, which is nearer than you thought. Nobody wants to hit an approach shot that appears to fly true to a blind green and then walk over the hill only to find a small pond in front of the green and no sign of your ball.

To alleviate these problems, you can obtain from the Independent Golfer's website *Caddienotes*, which are descriptions of 47 of the Highland and Island courses. Each *Caddienote* contains detailed information about the location of one course, including how to drive there, a general course description, and listing of amenities, the contact telephone number, and E-mail and website address. You will also find brief, detailed descriptions of each hole intended to help in your navigation. It would be impossible to include all the subtle details about fairway-roll and green-break that home players of these courses have come to know so well. Further, there is much that you can see on your own as you approach a hole that can inform your shot-making decisions. You don't need somebody telling you how to play every shot.

But you can learn in a *Caddienote* about the unseen burn that crosses the fairway 210 yards in front of the tee, about the best line over a hill to a blind fairway, or about the general shape of the green, whether it be saucer, sloped left, or plateau. There is no reason to be surprised when the ball that you purposely hit short in order to run up on the green sends up a splash of water from a pond in front of the green that you couldn't see when you hit your shot.

The focus of these *Caddienotes* tends to be primarily on tee and approach shots. To take an extreme example that illustrates the utility of this focus, we can look at Tiger Wood's 8-stroke victory in the 2000 British Open at St. Andrews. In his typically off-hand way, when asked after the Sunday round why he was so successful, he said, "I hit the ball well and some putts rolled in." Well, that may be the short of it, but it certainly doesn't go very far to explain his success. It goes without saying that much of his success was attributable to his phenomenal ball-striking ability as well as his excellent putting. But his real secret in 2000 was that he played St. Andrews as a links course should be played. Before the week of the Open, he spent considerable time with a few folks who know the Old Course well, mapping out a plan for its play. He worked with his coach on the particular shots that might be called for as he executed his plan. Then, during the tournament, he followed his plan to near perfection. He rarely hit driver off the tee, preferring to find the subtle paths down the fairway that would accept his ball and give the optimal roll in the best direction to the most advantageous location for his next shot. He went around the entire course without once hitting into a bunker, visible or hidden. He knew about how humps in a fairway could affect his perception of distance to the pin. He hit to blind greens on lines that he knew would not only hit the green, but would put his ball in the best position for a birdie putt. He hit approaches 30 yards short rather than three yards long, preferring to two-putt for a sure par rather than having to chip back to a green that he knew could not hold the ball close enough for an up-and-down. In short, "insider information" guided his decisions off the tee and towards the green. Combining that with his ability to execute the shots he wanted allowed him to blow away the competition in a tour de force that had no equal in the history of the Open.

None of us can hit the ball like Tiger, and maybe at times we hurt our games when we think we might try. But the principle of knowing about the course, especially about the tee shots and approaches, and trying to play within what the course gives us, is a sound one. Our difficulty comes when we walk onto a new course, especially one that plays so differently, as links courses do, from what we are accustomed to. In these cases, a *Caddienote* for the course you are playing will reduce a bit the handicap of unfamiliarity. In this way, your enjoyment of your round can be increased by the confidence that comes from knowing something about what is before you.

Please remember that all of this information must be integrated with your own abilities and with the playing conditions that you encounter. So, you see in the *Caddienote* for a particular course that there is a hidden burn crossing the fairway 210 yards from the tee box. How far can you confidently hit your drive? How about in a strong wind that is following you? In your face? Should you lay up? Should you chance carrying it and reap the reward of a much shorter second shot? Does the benefit outweigh the risk? These decisions, and the execution of the shots on which you decide, are still yours. It is hoped that the information in these *Caddienotes* will inform those decisions and thus make your round more enjoyable and, yes, maybe even lower your score a bit.

Caddienote descriptions are available for 47 courses in the Highlands and Islands, including:

Aigas Golf Course

Boat of Garten Golf Club

Brodick Golf Club

Carrbridge Golf Club

Dragon's Tooth Golf Course

Durness Golf Club

Fort William Golf Club

Gairloch Golf Club

Glencruitten (Oban) Golf Club

Grantown-on-Spey Golf Club

Inverarey Golf Club

Inverness Golf Club

Kingussie Golf Club

Lochgilphead Golf Club

Machrihanish Golf Club

Nairn Dunbar Golf Club

Newtonmore Golf Club

Royal Dornoch Golf Club –
    Championship

Shiskine Golf and Tennis Club

Strathpeffer Spa Golf Club

Tarbat Golf Club

Thurso Golf Club

Torvean Golf Club

Ullapool Golf Club

Alness Golf Club

Bonar Bridge Golf Club

Brora Golf Club

Corrie Golf Club

Dunaverty Golf Club

Fort Augustus Golf Club

Fortrose&Rosemarkie Golf Club

Giga Golf Club

Golspie Golf Club

Helmsdale Golf Club

Invergorden Golf Club

Isle of Skye Golf Club

Loch Ness Golf Course

Machri Hotel and Golf Links

Muir of Ord Golf Club

Nairn Golf Club

Reay Golf Club

Royal Dornoch Golf Club –
    Struie

Spean Bridge Golf Club

Tain Golf Club

Tarbert Golf Club

Tobermory Golf Club

Traigh Golf Course

In Appendix A, you can examine a sample *Caddienote*. This one is for the Golspie Golf Course, which is located about an hour and 20 minutes north of Inverness on the coast of the North Sea.

When you plan your golf trip to Scotland, you can obtain up-to-date *Caddienotes* for the courses you intend to play. Just go to The Independent Golfer's website at:

www.TheIndependentGolfer.com

Chapter 13
On Ye Go

What do you do when someone you are playing with is about to make a big mistake? Standing on the tee, you see that they have a driver in their hand on a hole where a well-struck drive will bring nothing but trouble. Do you stay silent as tragedy unfolds, or do you speak up to offer advice that was unsolicited and might or might not be welcome?

For the last three days, the skies of Inverness had been slate gray, low and wet. But the previous evening, as my wife and I walked the path along the river near the self-catering cottage we had rented for two weeks, the setting sun broke through the clouds with a golden light of possibility. After 32 years of marriage, Susan can detect when the always-optimistic golfer in me jumps to the prediction that maybe tomorrow would be a good golf day.

"Why don't you drive up and play Dornoch tomorrow? " she asked with a sly smile. "You can't leave without playing the Championship course once more." How did she know that was just what I was thinking?

That was all the encouragement I needed. Knowing that visiting golfers are discovering Dornoch and that, even in April, play can be heavy, I made a phone call to inquire about a start time for the following early afternoon. As it grows in popularity, Royal Dornoch has had to enforce an upper limit on handicaps to ensure that non-golfers don't encroach on golfers' play. The lady in the office said she would be happy to accept the information on the Southern California Golf Association's website concerning my handicap and that I should be on the tee at 2:30 tomorrow.

And so the next day, we drove the hour north from Inverness to the Royal Burgh of Dornoch and to the most magical links course in Scotland. Royal Dornoch is a golfer's dream. Everything is within two fairway-widths of the ocean. The wind-sculpted dunes, now covered with tough, tight links grasses, are shaped into natural fairways, tees, and greens over which generations of golfers have worked to better their scores. Donald Ross grew up on this course and learned the lessons that would, in later years, propel him to the top of the golf architecture world. The course is long by links standards (6514 yards, par 70). Calling for you to play every shot in your bag, it is as testing as any course in Scotland. In recent years, the town elders and members of the club have invested considerable time and money in maintenance and improvement so that their course has kept up with modern developments in the game. The result is an astonishing and, at times, breathtaking golf experience that ranks with the best in the world.

My wife was as eager to return to Dornoch as I. Susan anticipated seeing friends in the bookstore on the village square and petting Gilbert, the town cat, who can always be found asleep among the books in the store's front window. She would also take some time to walk the beaches that bordered the course. With luck, she might find another welk shell awash in the sand that she could add to her collection.

So I found myself, on a glorious day in April, standing on the tee of hole #8 –Dunrobin at Royal Dornoch and looking at my playing partner as he took out his driver. Roger, with whom I had been paired for the day, was a London businessman, a good golfer who had left a business meeting in Edinburgh to come up and play Royal Dornoch for his first time. Seeing on the card that Dunrobin is a 396-yard hole, he couldn't have known that everybody who has played it understands what happens to a good drive that flies directly over the black and white marker pole in the middle of the fairway. Invariably, will come to rest through the left-bending dogleg and in the rough which is all out of sight from the tee. The longer your drive is and the straighter it appears off the tee, the more difficult your second shot will be. Instead of a powerful drive, all you need is to carry and roll your ball 215 yards to reach the top edge of the large bank that angles across Dunrobin's fairway. From there, the ball will take on a life of its own, bounding onward, down the bank and into a large flat area from which a straightforward 130-yard iron will get you home.

Roger, with driver in hand, was facing potential disaster. Should I point out Dunrobin's cunning trap? Keeping my mouth shut, I pushed forward to tee my ball up first, waving my 3-iron about like I was practicing fly fishing. Lucky enough to hit a decent shot, I was treated to seeing my ball bounce twice and then disappear over the bank. I knew it would end in prime position for my approach.

"You hit an iron," he observed. "It's a pretty broad fairway. Worried about going left or right?"

"Nope. 215 roll out is all you need here," I replied.

I was relieved to see Roger, after a short hesitation, put back his driver in favor of a 5-wood that he then hit well. My moment of moral conflict was over and we moved on, enjoying a growing camaraderie built on our mutual appreciation for golf played where it has seemingly always been played along this lovely and wild Highland coast.

The rest of the round was as enchanting as you might expect. The course held its own, as it always does, yielding occasional pars and then reminding us that success in golf is not something to achieve but only to pursue. As we played the latter holes, a bank of dark clouds moved in from the north with an apron of pewter gray that hung to the sea . Though the squall missed us, we could see umbrellas sprouting in the distance along the holes we had recently played. The brisk wind brought a clean sense of freshness off the sea. The sky above us showed occasional patches of blue among billowing white and grey. Life was good.

Afternoons like these are what define golf for the Independent Golfer in Scotland. They happen when you have the freedom to play when and where you want, to spontaneously change plans and act on a whim. They are so memorable because they are set amid the wild and wondrous scenery of the Highlands' mountains, oceans, forests, and small and ancient villages. But most importantly, they happen on the courses that gave birth to golf and that retain the unspoiled character of this simple game that has so many levels of experience and meaning. Here is where golf is meant to be played, where the greats of the game have always found their purest challenge.

The most wonderful message of all is that you can make afternoons like these happen for yourself and your golfing partners. You don't need somebody else to plan your itinerary, to schedule your days, and to control your golfing life. You can take charge, do the planning, keep your costs affordable, and enjoy an Independent Golfer's dream, a trip to the Highlands and Islands of Scotland.

As the Scots say, "On ye go!"

Golspie Golf Club

A James Braid Golf Course

LOCATION:
Turn right off the A9 toward the sea at the south end of the town of Golspie.

DESCRIPTION:
TYPE – Links, Heathland, Parkland
NUM OF HOLES – 18
  Par 5 = 1
  Par 4 = 12
  Par 3 = 5
PAR – 68
LENGTH – 5693
COST – Round = £25 weekday, £35 weekend
    Day Ticket = £25 weekday, £35 weekend
AMENITIES – Clubhouse w/ Bar and Food, Locker Room w/ Shower, Pro Shop, Club & Pull Cart Rental, Putting Green.

CONTACTS:
TELEPHONE: 01408 633266
E-MAIL: info@golspie-golf-club.co.uk
WEBSITE: www.golspie-golf-club.co.uk

FEATURES:

The people at Golspie claim that their course offers three kinds of play: links, heathland and parkland. In fact, all of Golspie plays like a classic links course. It does feature a few holes, labeled heathland, that are cut through beautiful fields of heather and gorse and two holes adjacent to a Scotch pine forest that are labeled parkland. Still, the geography of all the fairways and greens and the nature of the grasses that cover them make Golspie play like a links course which is, of course, Golspie's strength.

Golspie's generally broad fairways are kind to the high handicapper while it's risk/reward choices challenge the best. It is a relatively long course by Scottish standards. Though it's overall length is just under 5700 yards, it is a par 70 with only one par 5. That makes the par-4's quite long; five of them are between 400 and 437 yards. More importantly, Golspie offers variation and subtlety. It repeatedly asks you to make decisions as to how you will play. You can take the bold line with its inherent risk and potential reward or you can be more cautious in an effort to protect your card from disaster. Golspie is cleaver, hiding its secrets behind patches of heather or in unseen undulations in the fairway. It is an imaginative course, presenting you with greens that are sauciered, domed, hidden beyond grass-tufted hills or even two-tiered. Above all, it is a course of differences. Each hole offers something new. Each shot requires thought and even a bit of imagination.

The Golspie course was founded in 1889 on the links land south of the town and evolved over the years with input from the legendary James Braid. It seems to crouch under the eminence of Ben Bhraggie, the dominating mountain just inland that bears the much-larger-than-life statue of the First Duke of Sutherland.

FINDING YOUR WAY:

NOTE: Blue disk distance markers are placed 150 yards from the FRONT of each green. Stroke saver booklets are available in the pro shop.

- #1 – "Backies" 386 yds.
  The first hole starts out going east, toward the town. Though the landing area is very generous, it slopes away to the right

while the hole doglegs left. The line down the left, toward the soccer goals in the distance, is best. A mistake to the right is no problem while the rock fence on the left is OB. A large green accepts your approach shot with no problems.

- #2 – "Kirk" 165 yds..
  The first of Golspie's five 3-pars. Each offers something different. The green here is protected by four bunkers, only one of which is visible from the tee. The hump in the front part of the green can kick your shot in any direction. Landing your ball toward the back of the green solves this uncertainty.

- #3 – "Shore" 352 yds.
  The big drive (over 230 yards) needs to go down the right to avoid a large area of rough that juts from the left into the fairway. Anything shorter can be anywhere in the fairway.

- #4 – "Gully" 522 yds.
  Golspie gives you a choice here. If your first two shots are long and accurate, you can carry the 30 yard wide rough-filled gully that bisects the fairway 120 yards in front of the green and be rewarded with a short chip and putt for a possible birdie. But hitting long is taking a chance. The much safer path is to hit your tee shot no more than 190, thus taking the large grass bunker out of play. Your 2nd shot needs to travel no more than 200 yards to come up short of the gully. You then have a short iron shot to the green. You decide.

- #5 – "Sahara" 287 yds.
  Again, a choice off the tee. A big drive that carries over the hump in the right of the fairway will run far forward leaving you no more than 50 yards to the green. The safer tee shot is about 180 yards long and still gives you a 95 shot to the landing area in front of the green. The ball will run down onto the large, flat green.

- #6 – "Saucer" 146 yds.
  The character of this par-3 comes from it's bunkers and it's large dish-shaped green. The two bunkers you see are well in front and should not present any difficulty. The four unseen bunkers, especially the three on the right edge of the green, are another story. Beware. This undulating green with its large hump on the left makes for interesting putting.

Remember to walk back down to the left toward the ocean to get to the 7th tee.

- #7 – "Fleet" 279 yds.
  Again, do you want to take a chance or play it safe. Depending upon the conditions, a big drive will carry beyond the black/white marker poll leaving a short iron shot to the green. But a tee shot just short of the marker can leave a blind shot with an awkward, uphill lie. The safe tee shot runs to a stop only 160 yards out but still leaves a reasonable approach of about 120 yards to be hit from a flat lie. It will still be blind so, as you walk off the tee, mark the line your next shot should take with the hills beyond and then with the top of the bank in front of you. The green has a classic Golspie subtlety, a deep swale that runs across most of the front of the green.

- #8 – "Wood" 400 yds.
  Here you depart the links appearance and enter the heathland with gorse and heather lining the fairway. Golspie sets its trap for you here in the form of an almost invisible ridge that crosses the fairway diagonally from near right to far left. The key off the tee is to carry this ridge in order to get a big roll for a good distance. The ball that lands short will be turned left and not allowed to roll out. The near right requires only 180 yards to carry the ridge, but it is off line to the green that is down the dogleg to the left. Further, a shot down the extreme right will clear the ridge but run into the rough. The far left requires a 220 yard carry, and gets you going in the proper direction. But this hole isn't finished with you. Even a good drive leaves a long approach shot to a green protected by patches of heather on each side 30 yards in front and a cleverly hidden bunker on the front right of the green. Any question why this is the #5 handicap hole?

- #9 – "Paradise" 408 yds.
  Hit your drive as far as you can, keeping it in the fairway and out of the heather on the left and right. You'll need the length on this #1 handicap hole. Your second, long shot should be to the right side of the green. The white triangle marker behind the green gives a good line. If you must be short, be right for a good opening to the green.

- #10 – "Lochy" 140 yds.
  What a beautiful setting for a hole! Scotch pines on the left,

two ponds set in a field of heather in front with Ben Bhraggie
as a backdrop in the distance. The only trouble on this hole is
hitting too long.

- #11 – "Tinker's Camp" 323 yds.
  Another beautiful setting! You hit out of a Scotch pine forest
  into a large fairway surrounded by heather and gorse. The
  large patch of gorse that comes in from the right at the far end
  of the landing area is 225 yards out and thus a good target
  for all but the long hitters. The longer drive much chance a
  line down the left, near the heather, to take advantage of the
  fairway's roll.

- #12 – "Table" 323 yds.
  The drive is made easy by a large landing area, the best line
  being at the lonely tree to the right of the green, but the
  green is this hole's challenge. It is raised on a high plateau and
  protected by bunkers left and right. From a good position in
  the fairway the green will accept a bump and run approach up
  between the bunkers.

- #13 – "Cup" 311 yds.
  Another good driving hole. The best line here is left of center,
  This green is again protected by bunkers, this time four, but, as
  with #12, a bump and run approach can succeed nicely.

- #14 – "Fields" 425 yds.
  Off the tee you are given a generous landing area, but don't
  drift too far left or right. Hidden from view are two sand and
  two grass bunkers on the right and two sand bunkers on the left
  placed well to catch the errant drive. You have a long approach
  shot to reach the green near the clubhouse.
  Now, walk downhill toward the sea to the #15 tee.

- #15 – "Tattie Pits" 410 yds.
  The trick on your drive is to avoid the grass bunkers (tattie pits
  or potato gardens) that march across the fairway and then up
  the left side, staring about 160 yards from the tee. The best
  line is up the right as anything center or left will feed left into
  trouble. Your long approach shot should be right, too, or it will
  feed left into trouble.

- #16 – "Cairngorms" 167 yds.
  What a testing par-3! It presents you with a two-tiered green
  protected by two bunkers on the left and big trouble on the

right and long. Now's the time for a career mid-iron shot.

- #17 – "Sahara Back" 212
  The second of two 3-pars in a row, if you complete these two in 6 you should be very happy with yourself. The white triangle behind the green is your target.

- #18 – "Drum Brae" 437 yds.
  Golspie saves the longest par-4 for last. The longer the drive, the easier it will be to get home in two but, as always on Golspie, length brings risk, this time in the form of deep rough pits on the left and right of the landing area. Your second shot flies over the black/white marker at the top of the hill and will be fortunate to carry all the way to the green. For most, an up-and-down is the only hope for par.

Index

A

Aberdeen 74, 97
Adams, Rev. Dr. Robert 122
Afternoon Tea 109
Aigas Golf Course 33, 50, 81
Alexander Matheson - "Pipey" 39
Alness Golf Course 81
Alternatives to Rental Cars 94
AMK Self Drive 88
Arnold Clark 88
Arnold Palmer 11
Arran, Isle of 94
Atlantic Ocean 71

B

baguettes 107
baked potatoes 107
ballot – for Old Course 75
Barra, Isle of 85
Battlefields 135
BBC 127
Beauly River 33
Bed and Breakfast 7, 73, 76, 77, 97, 98, 99, 100, 103
Black Isle 71
Bloody Butcher. See Duke of Cumberland

Boat of Garten Golf Club 75, 81
Bonnie Prince Charlie 135, 136
Braid, James 13, 17, 147
Braveheart 21
British Open 9, 16, 59, 150
Brodick 94
Brora Golf Club 2, 17, 57, 75, 77, 82, 132
Buggy 40, 41
Burns, Robert 110

C

Cairnbaan Hotel 76
Caledonian Canal 82
Caledonian MacBrayne 85, 94
Campbeltown 16
canoe/kayaking 133
Cape Wrath 71
Carnegie Shield 62, 63
Carnoustie Golf Course 4, 11, 61
Castles 131
Ceilidh (KAY-lee) 141
Chanonry Ness 19
Chippies 108
Citylink Bus 95
Clachneart Toss 128
Clubhouse 64, 109

Club Covering 117
Club Membership 12, 64
Coll, Isle of 85
Colonsay, Isle of 85
Competition 34
Corrie Golf Club 94
Courtesy on the Course 46
Cromarty Firth 56, 71
Cruden Bay Golf Course
    74
Culloden Battlefield 135
Curbies 92
Customs of Play in Scotland
    23

D

DCH Scotland Ltd. 88
democratization of golf
    122
Dinner 110
Distance Markers 50
Distillery Visits 137
Donald Ross 102, 147
Dornoch Village 81, 82,
    102, 103, 130
Dragon's Tooth Golf
    Course 20, 83, 135
Dress on the Course 45
Driving in Scotland 88
Drunk Driving 94
Duchess of Bedford 109
Duke of Cumberland 135
Duke of Sutherland 134
Dunaverty Golf Club 83
Dunollie Castle 85

Dunrobin Castle 132, 141
Durness Golf Club 3, 71,
    72, 83, 84

E

"Explore Scotland" pack-
    ages 95
East Lothian 119
Edinburgh 12, 51, 75, 88
Eileen Donan Castle 131
Elie Golf Club 45
Entering an Open 61
en suite 99

F

Falconry 127
Featheies 120
Ferries 94
Finding Your Way 149,
    150, 151
Firth of Forth 45
Fishing 133
Fish and chips 107, 110,
    111
Forgan, Robert 124
Forres Golf Course 76
Fortrose and Rosemarkie
    Golf Club 18, 50
Fort Augustus 127, 130
Fort George 19
Fort William Golf Club 48,
    50, 83, 135
Foursome 23, 24, 37
Fully Licensed 66
Full Scottish Breakfast 97

G

Gairloch Golf Club 83,
    131, 133, 134
Gairloch village 133
George II 135
Glasgow 12, 79, 80, 88,
    132, 146
Glencruitten Golf Club 85,
    97
Gleneagles Golf Course 55
Glenmorangie Whiskey
    Distillery 55
Glen Afric 33
Glen Coe 135
Glen Eagles Golf Course
    11
Golf Magazine 14
Golspie Golf Course 2, 57,
    75, 82, 132
Golspie Village 141
Grantown-on-Spey Golf
    Course 81
Great Glen 82
Guest Houses 100, 103
Gullane #1 Golf Course
    24, 75
Gutta-percha 122

H

Haggis 106, 110
Half & Half 108
Hammer Throw 128
Handa Island 29
Haskell ball 123
Heathland 32

Helmsdale Golf Club. 68
Henry Stuart, Lord Darnley
    119
Het Kloven 119
Highland Clearances 132
Highland Games 73, 127,
    130
Highland Scotch Beef 110
High Tea 110
Hiking. See hill walking
Hill-Walking 133
History of Scotland 131
Holinshead's *Chronicles* 137
Honourable Company of
    Edinburgh Golfers 23,
    119
Hotels 100
Hub Strategy 77, 78

I

Inveraray Golf Club 19, 83
Invergorden Golf Club 81
Inverness, City of 18, 35,
    56, 71, 74, 81 103
Inverness Golf Course 81,
    131, 135
Irn-Bru 108
Island Hopscotch 94
Island Rover 94
Islay, Isle of 83, 85, 94
Isle of Skye Golf Club 84,
    131

J

James Graham, the Marquis
    of Montrose 119

James II 119
James VIII 135
Jubilee Golf Course 59

K

Kingsmill Hotel 74
Kings Acre Golf Course 51
Kingussie Golf Club 36, 81
Kintyre 14, 83
Kyle of Lochalsh 131

L

Ladies Days 57
Lager Tops 108
Links Golf 24-32
Links Grasses 28, 29
Lismore 85
Lochgilphead 76, 83
Loch Fyne 19
Loch Lomond 11
Loch Ness 82
Loch Ness Golf Course 81,
    131, 1355
Longnoses 121
Lords of Lorne 85
Lunch 106-108

M

MacBeth 81
MacDougal Clan 85
Machrie Hotel and Golf
    Course 57, 76, 83, 94
Machrihanish Golf Club
    14, 15, 16, 17, 57, 76,
    83

Macwilliam, Norman 36
Madonna 83
Making Reservations 103
Malt Whiskies 67
Marcliff at Pitofels 74
Mary Queen of Scots 119
Match Play 37
Medal Tees 51, 53
Montrose Golf Course 74
Moray Firth 19, 82, 127
Moray Golf Course 76
Muirfield Golf Course 11,
    23, 24, 55, 61
Muir of Ord Golf Course
    81, 135
Mull, Isle of 85, 94
Music 139

N

Nairn Golf Club 4, 27, 35,
    55, 57, 66, 74-76, 81
    135
Nairn Dunbar Golf Club
    57, 81, 1351
Nairn Dunbar Open 63
National Historical Trust
    131
National Nature Reserve 83
Newtonmore Golf Course
    81
Niblick 121, 123
Nicholas, Jack 11
North Atlantic 115
North Sea 14, 71, 82, 115,
    132

O

Oakland Hills 102
Oban 81, 83, 97, 103
Official Guide to Golf in Scotland 38, 120
Old Course Hotel 74
Old Tom Morris 13, 15, 22, 56, 147
Other Styles of Scottish Golf 32

P

Paganica 119
Par 36, 37
Parkland 32, 33
Pavement Markings 92
Peat Bog Faeries 139
Pentland Firth 25
Pinehurst No. 2 102
Playing the Well-Known Courses 59
Playing Through 44
Ploughman's Lunch 107
Pony Treking 133
Prestwick Golf Club 4, 61, 119
Prestwick St. Nicholas Golf Club 90
Pub Lunch 106

R

Railroad 125
Rain Clothing 116, 117
Reay Golf Club 25, 83, 84
Rental Car 87

River Spey 36
Rob Roy MacGregor 21
Rock Climbing 133
Romans 119
Roundabout 90
Roundabouts 89
Royal Aberdeen Golf Course 74
Royal Burgh of Dornoch 44
Royal Dornoch Golf Club 1, 4, 14, 15, 16, 17, 24, 34, 39, 57, 62, 74, 75, 76, 81, 82, 102, 127, 132
Royal Dornoch – Struie 29, 44
Royal Troon Golf Course 4, 11, 55, 61
Ryder Cup 17, 59

S

Sailing 133
Sandside Bay 25
ScotRail 95
Scotti 136
Scottish Cooked Full Breakfast 105
Scottish Four-ball 37
Scottish Golf Union 34
Scottish Land Reform Act 135
Self-Catering 101, 102
Seminole 102
Shandy 108
Sheaf Toss 128

Sheep Dog 127
Sheep Wallows 30
Shiskin Golf and Tennis
    Club 94
Signage 92
Skye, Isle of 133
Small Hotel 73
Society of the St. Andrews
    Golfers 119
South Uist, Isle of 85
Speed Limit, National 93
Spoons 121
St. Andrews - Old Course
    4, 11, 42, 47, 59, 74, 75,
    145, 150
St. Andrews – Balgove
    Course 59
St. Andrews – Eden Course
    59
St. Andrews – Jubilee
    Course 74
St. Andrews – Strathtyrum
    Course 59
St. Andrews Links Trust 55,
    59
Stevenson, Robert Lewis
    21
Sticky Toffee Pudding 110
Strathpeffer Spa Golf Club
    3, 71, 72, 73, 81, 113,
    114
Stroke Savers 149
Sutherland Pipe Band 141
Swilkin Burn 145

T

Tain Golf Club 2, 30, 31,
    56, 75-77, 81, 132
Tarbert Golf Club 83
Telephone (calling Scotland)
    58
The Old Course Experience
    60
The Royal and Ancient
    Golf Club of St.
    Andrews 23
Three Sisters of Kintail 71
Thurso Golf Club 84
Time of Play 38
Tiree, Isle of 85
Tobermory Golf Club 46,
    85, 94, 111
Torvean Golf Club 81, 131
Traigh Golf Club 131
Turnberry Golf Club 11,
    55, 61

U

Ullapool Golf Club 83
United States Golf Associa-
    tion 23, 34, 42, 59
Urquhart Castle 131

V

Van de Velde, Jean 11
VisitScotland 101, 103, 140

W

Wallace, william 21

Watson, Tom 47
Weather 113
Wee Yellow Book 63
Weight Toss for Height 128
Whiskey 136, 138
Whiskey Mac 108
Wick Golf Club 67
Windsurfing 133
Woods, Tiger 150
World War II submarine 45